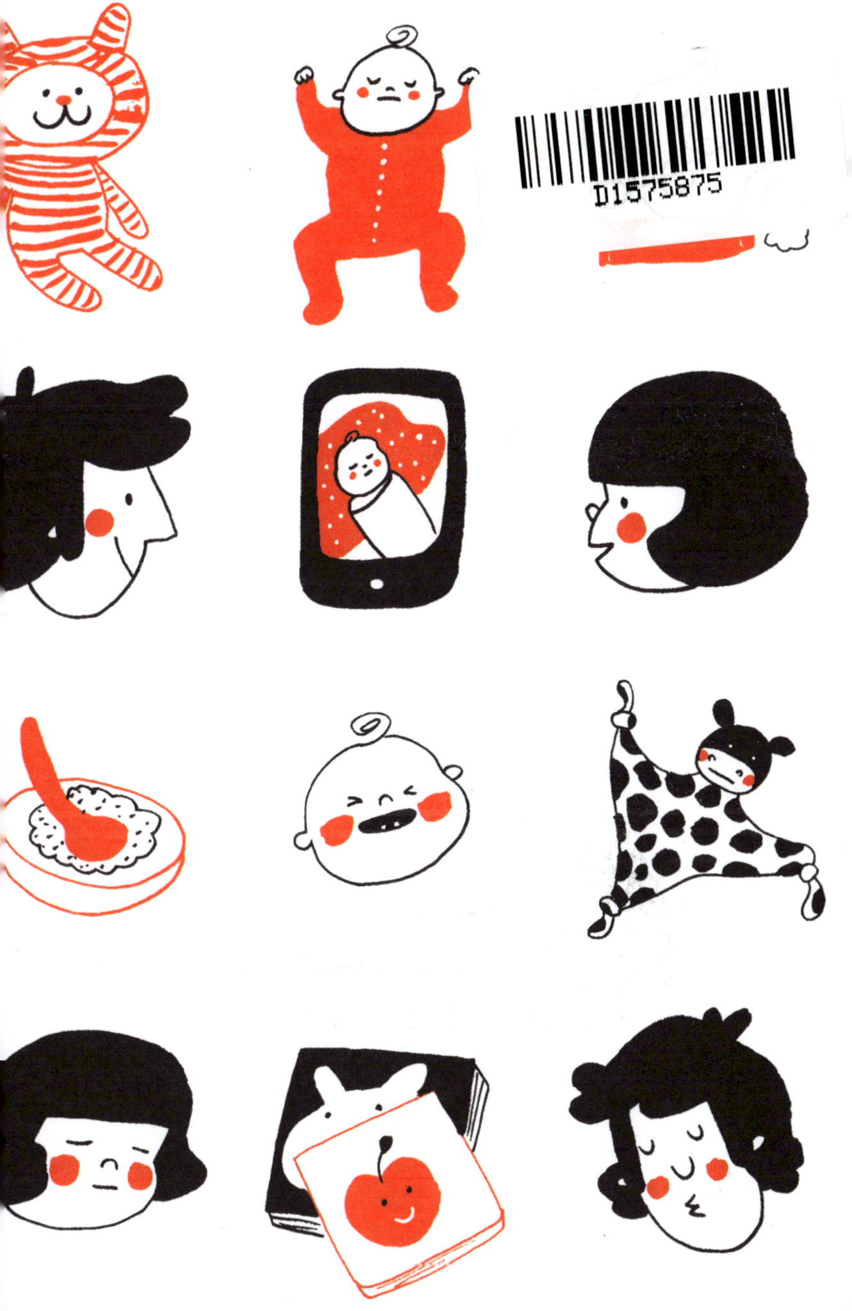

Baby

A Soppy Story

Philippa Rice

Andrews McMeel
PUBLISHING®

for Robin

and Luke

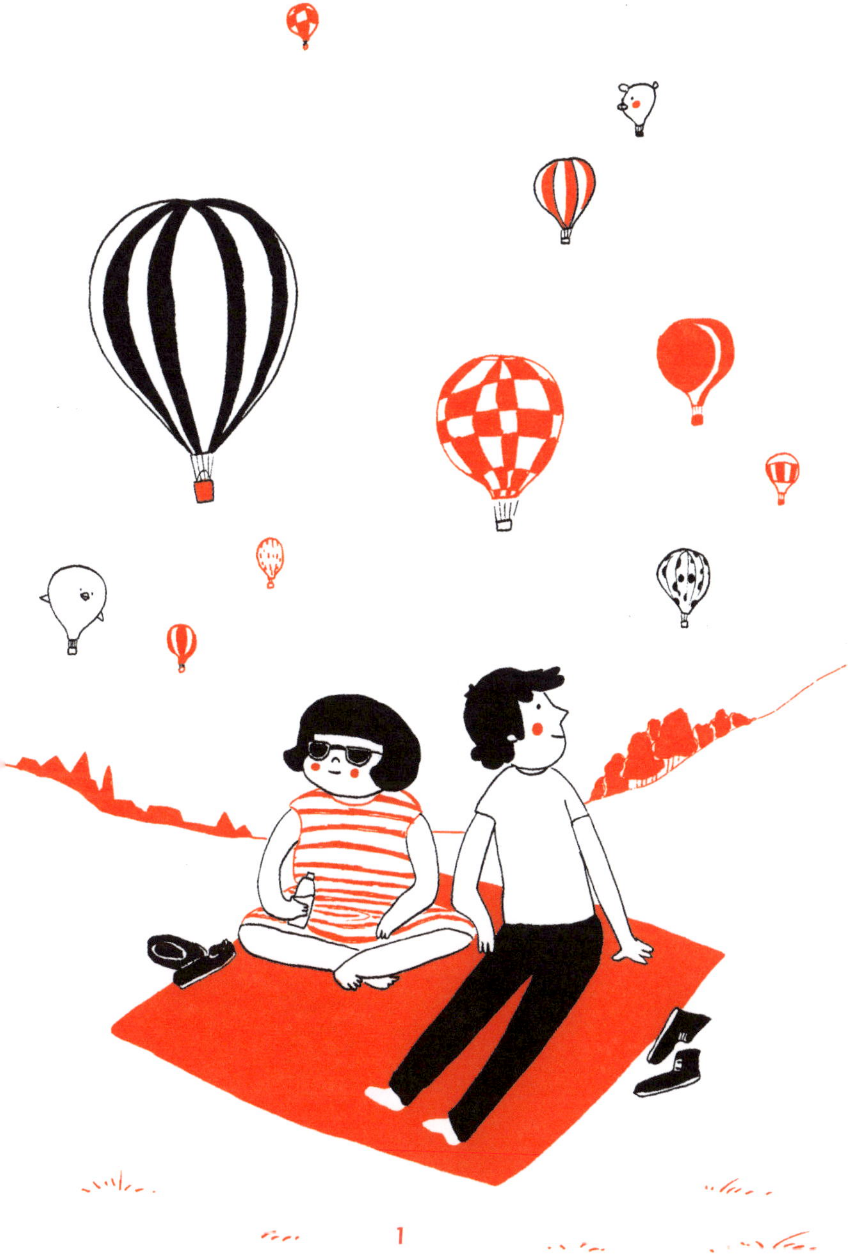

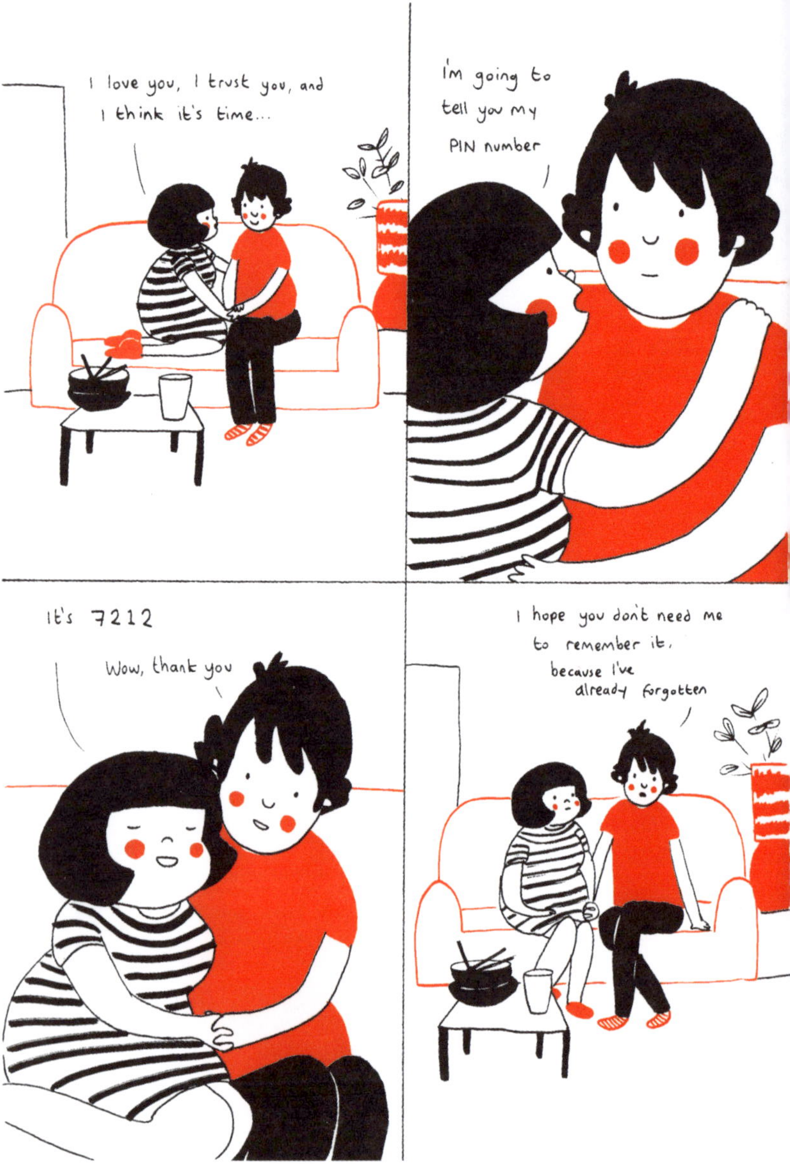
I love you, I trust you, and I think it's time...
I'm going to tell you my PIN number
It's 7212
Wow, thank you
I hope you don't need me to remember it,
because I've already forgotten

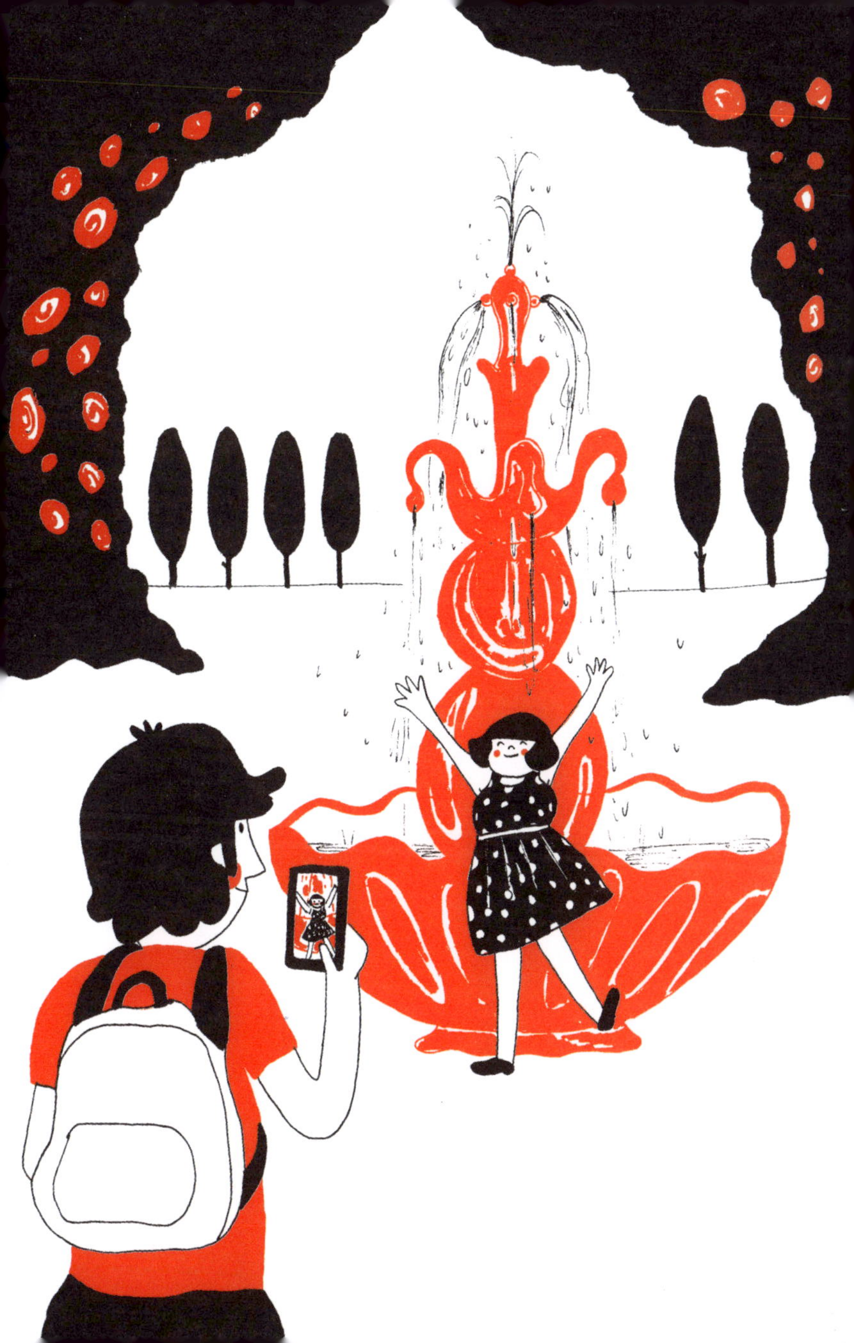

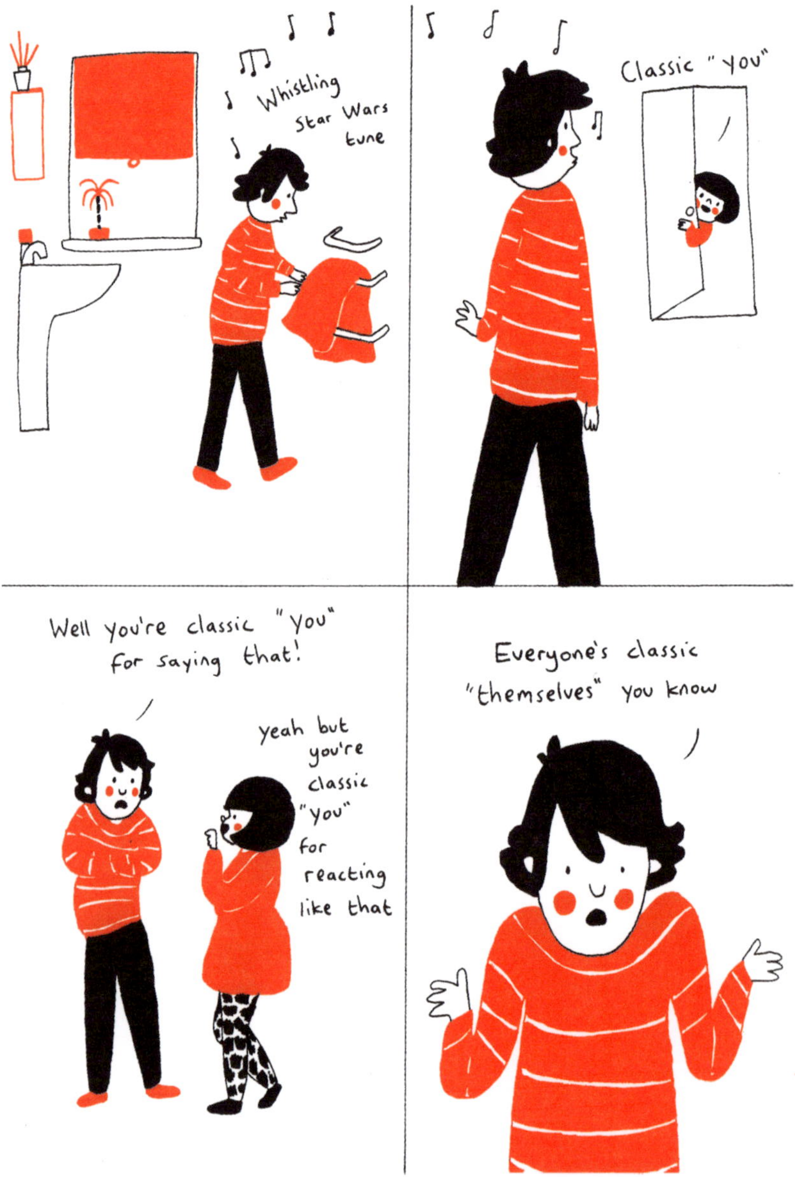
Whistling Star Wars tune
Classic "you"
Well you're classic "you" for saying that!
yeah but you're classic "you" for reacting like that
Everyone's classic "themselves" you know

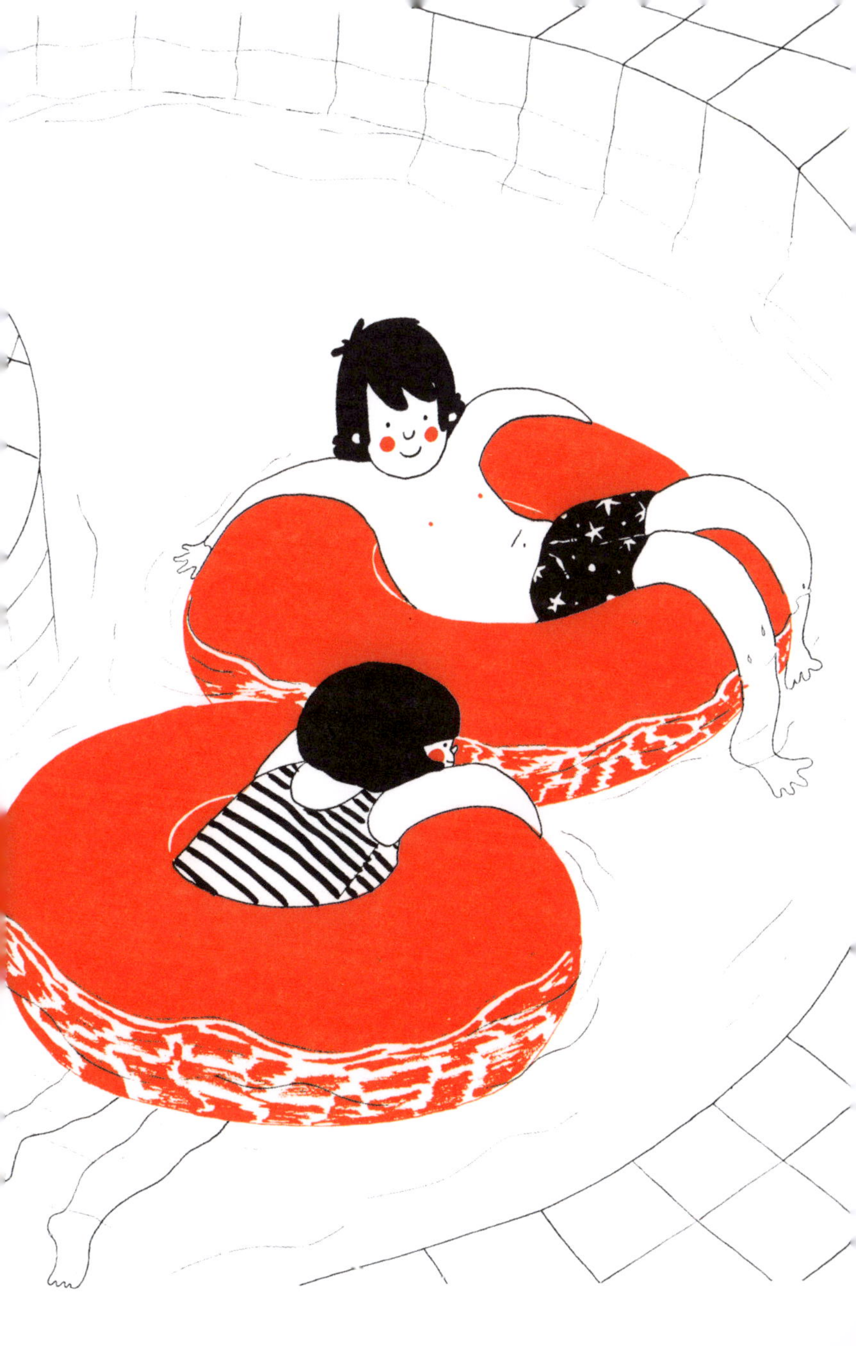

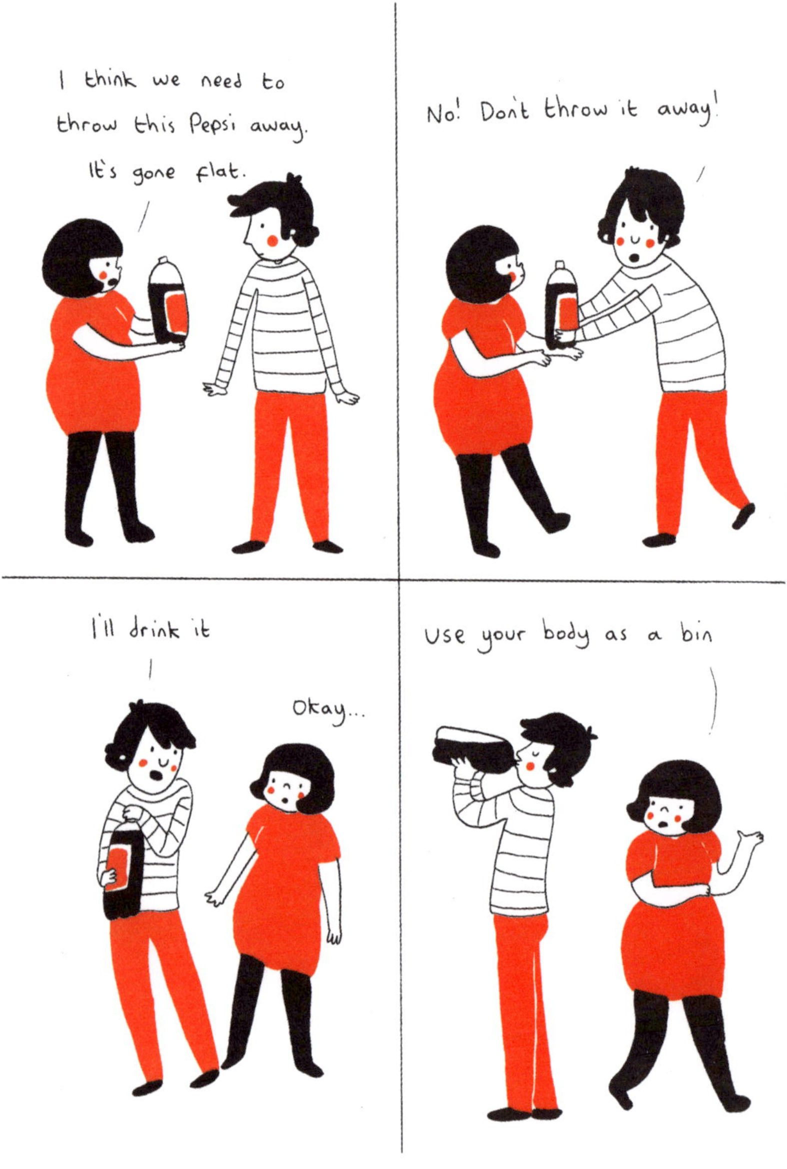
I think we need to throw this Pepsi away. It's gone flat.
No! Don't throw it away!
I'll drink it
Okay...
Use your body as a bin

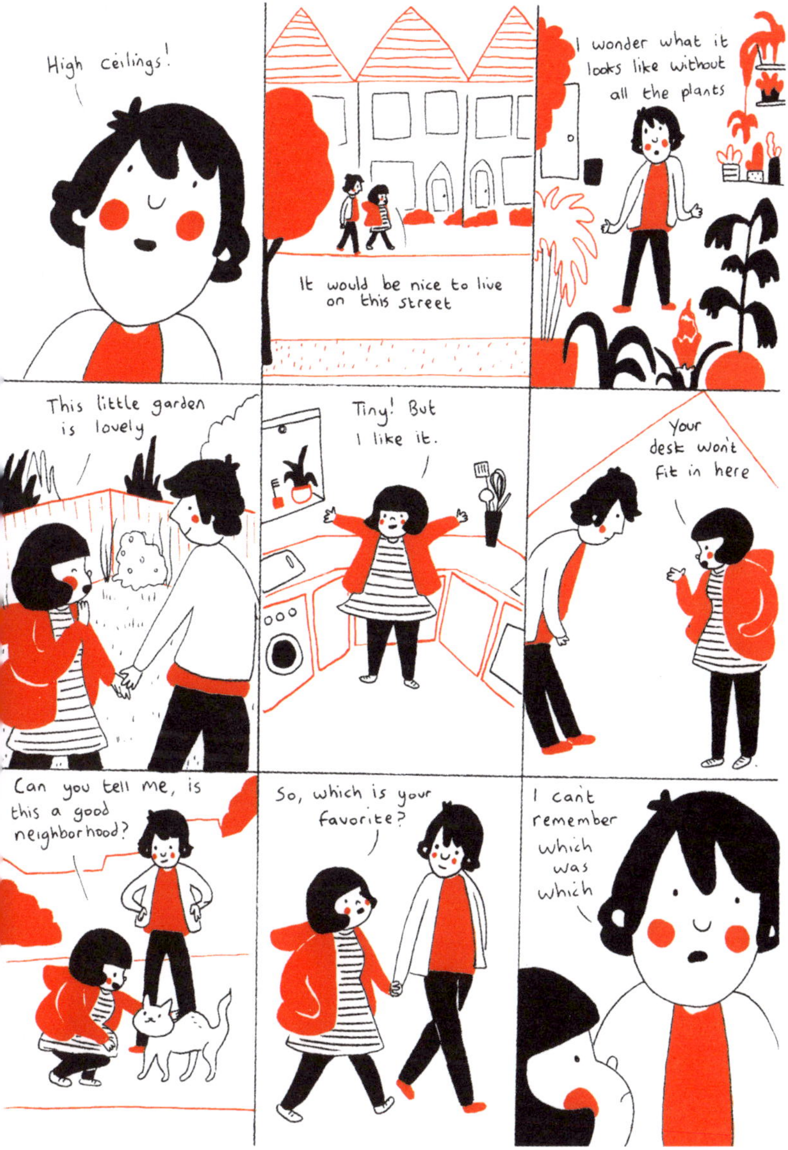

High ceilings!
It would be nice to live on this street
I wonder what it looks like without all the plants
This little garden is lovely
Tiny! But I like it.
Your desk won't fit in here
Can you tell me, is this a good neighborhood?
So, which is your favorite?
I can't remember which was which

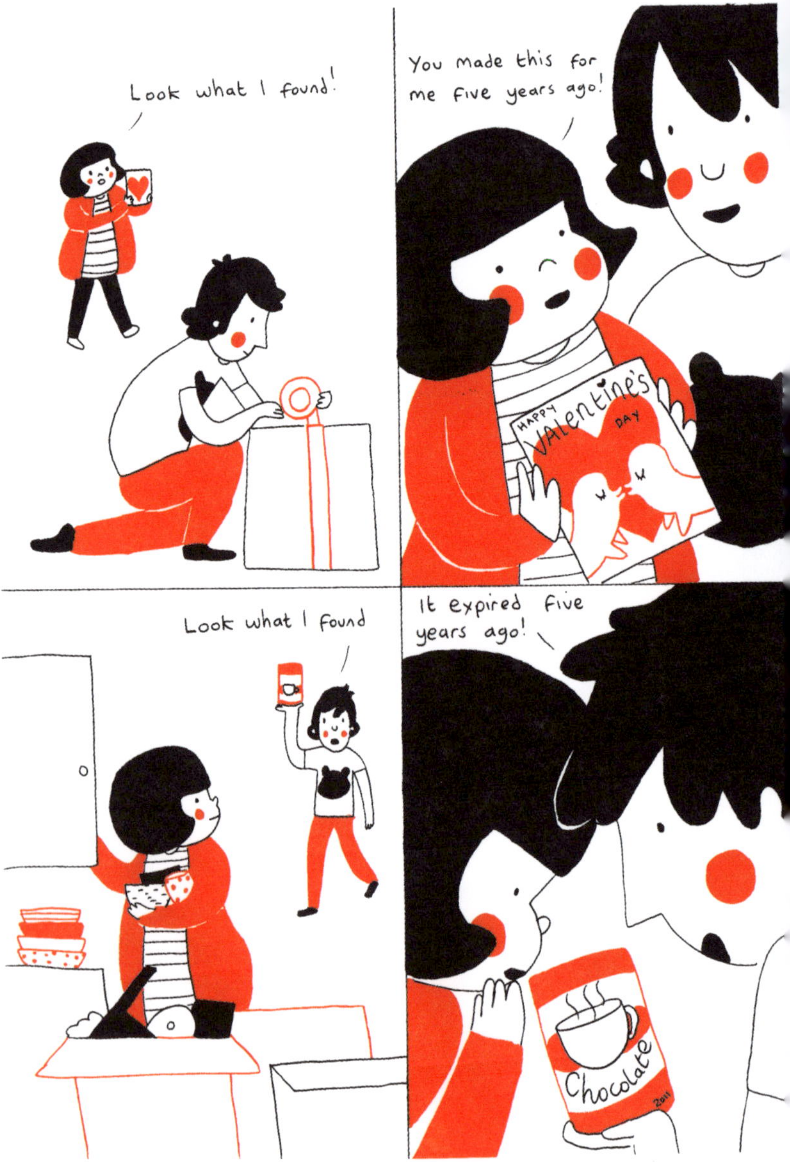
Look what I found!
You made this for me five years ago!
HAPPY Valentine's DAY
Look what I found
It expired five years ago!
Chocolate
2011

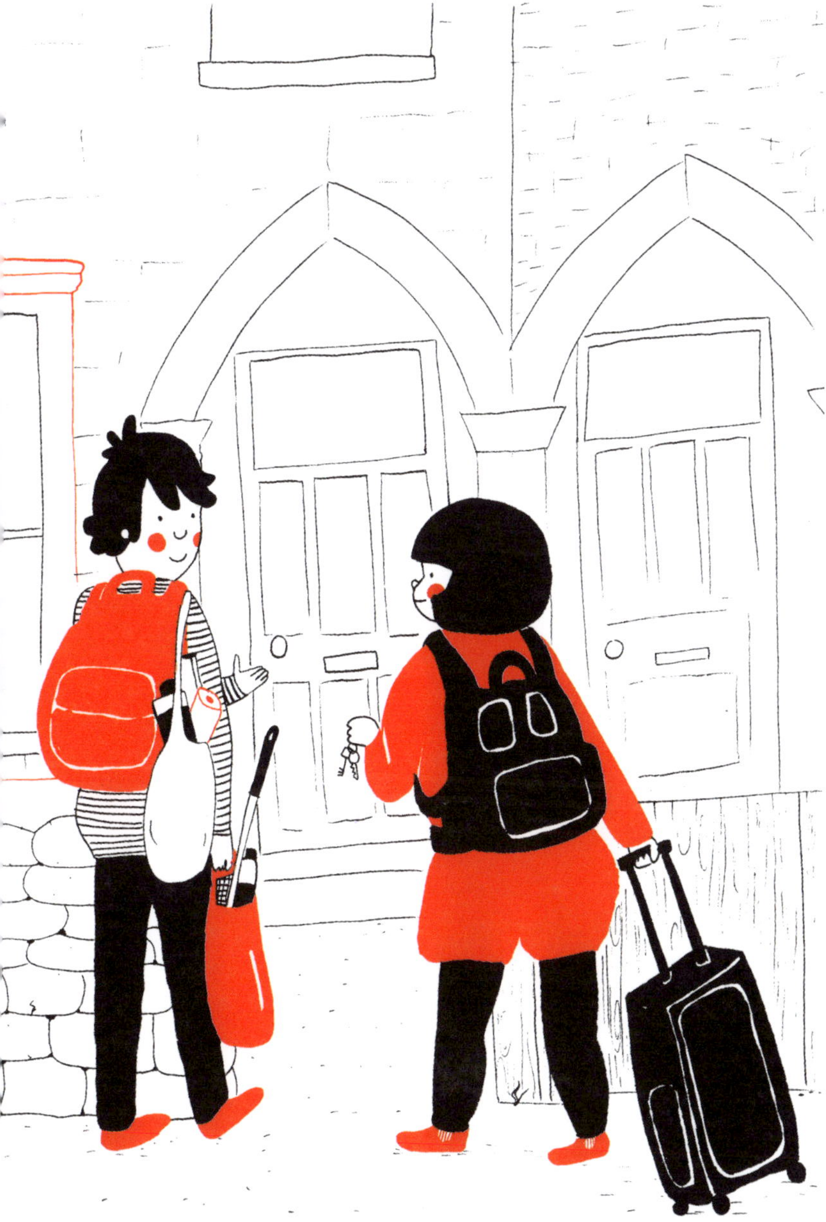

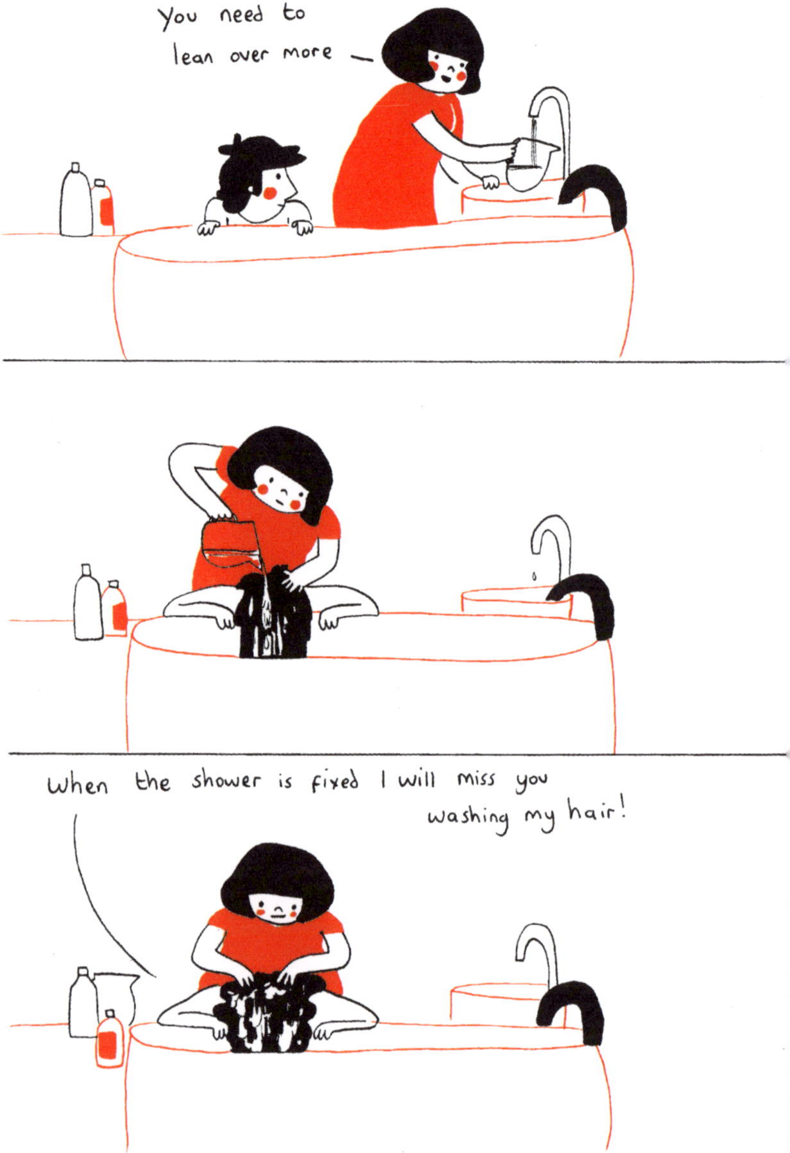
You need to lean over more
When the shower is fixed I will miss you washing my hair!

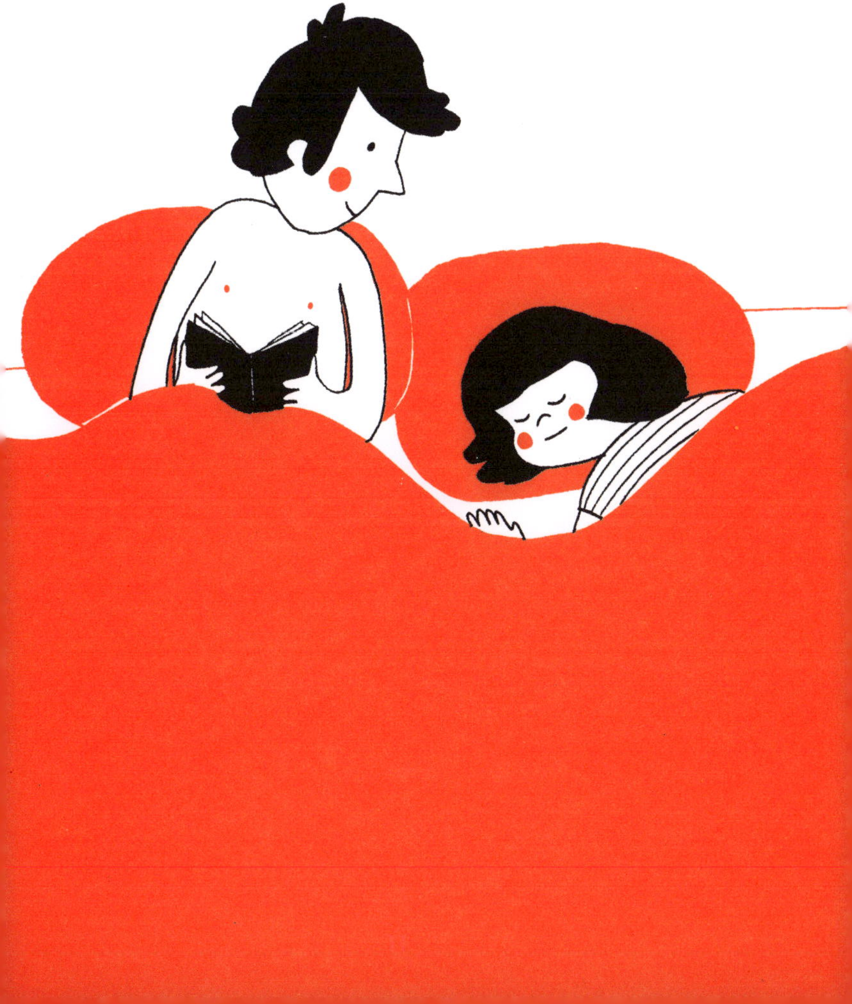

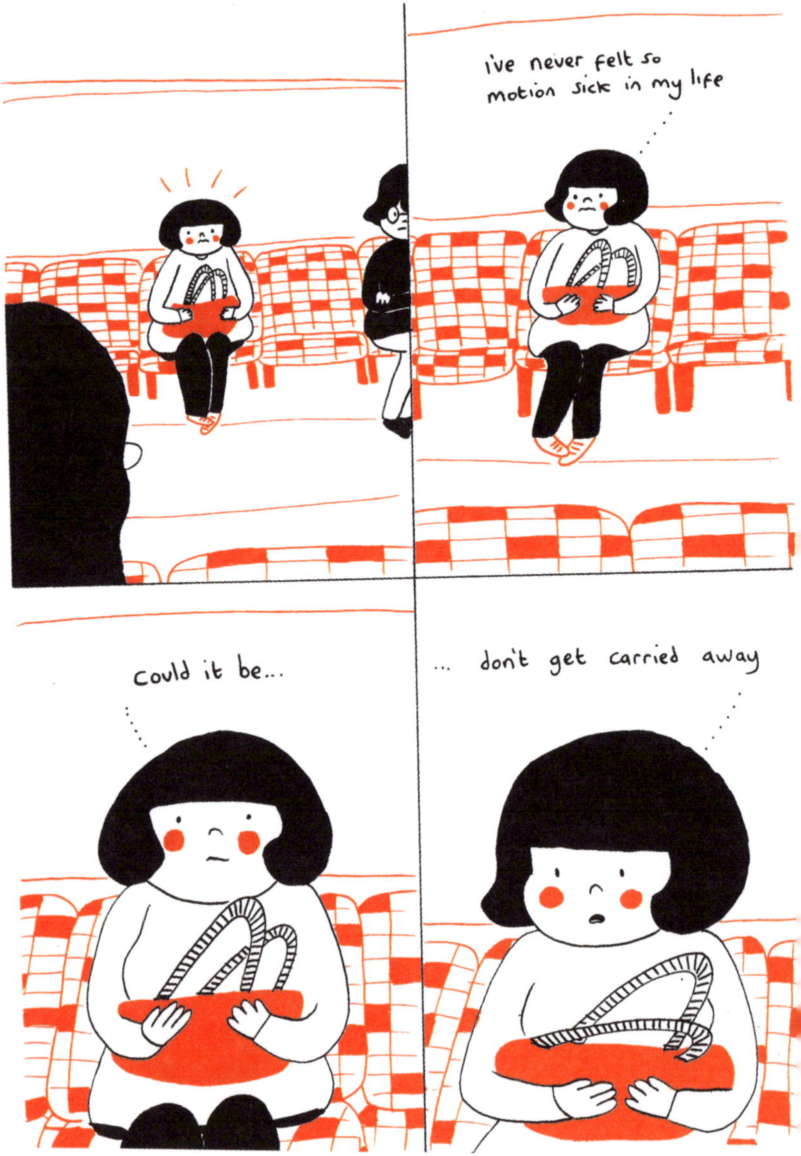
i've never felt so motion sick in my life
could it be...
... don't get carried away

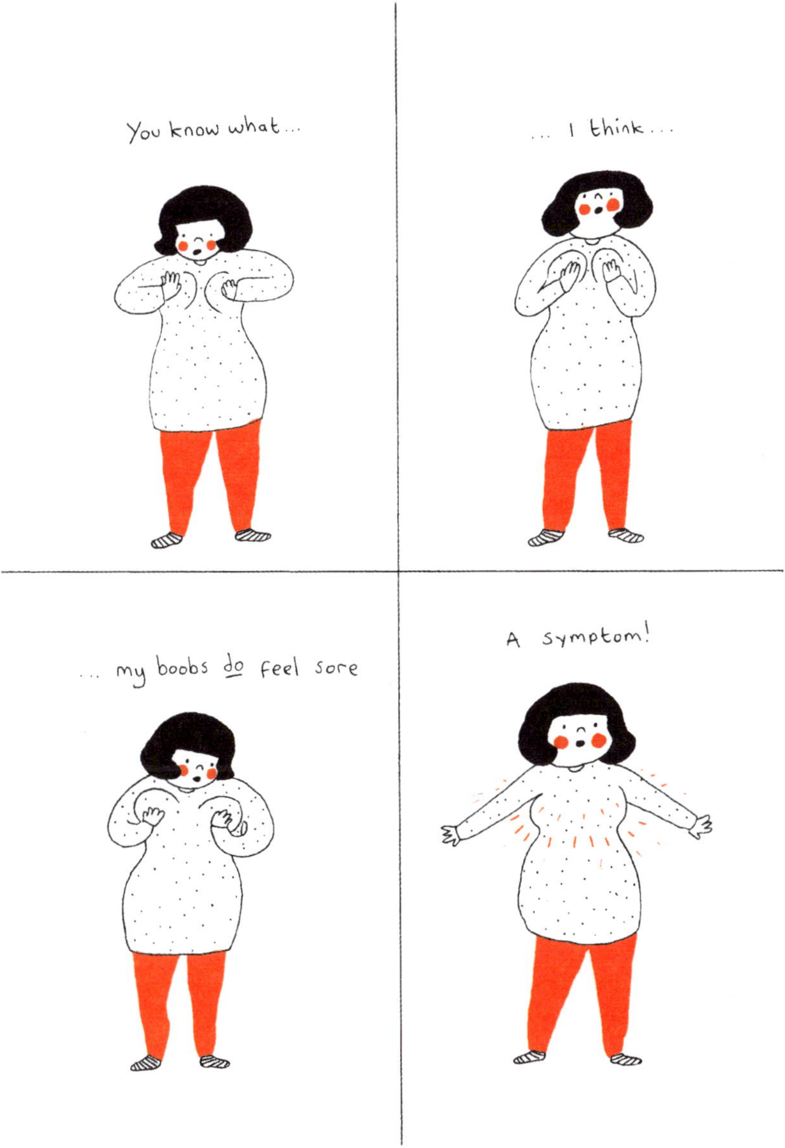
You know what...
... I think...
... my boobs do feel sore
A symptom!

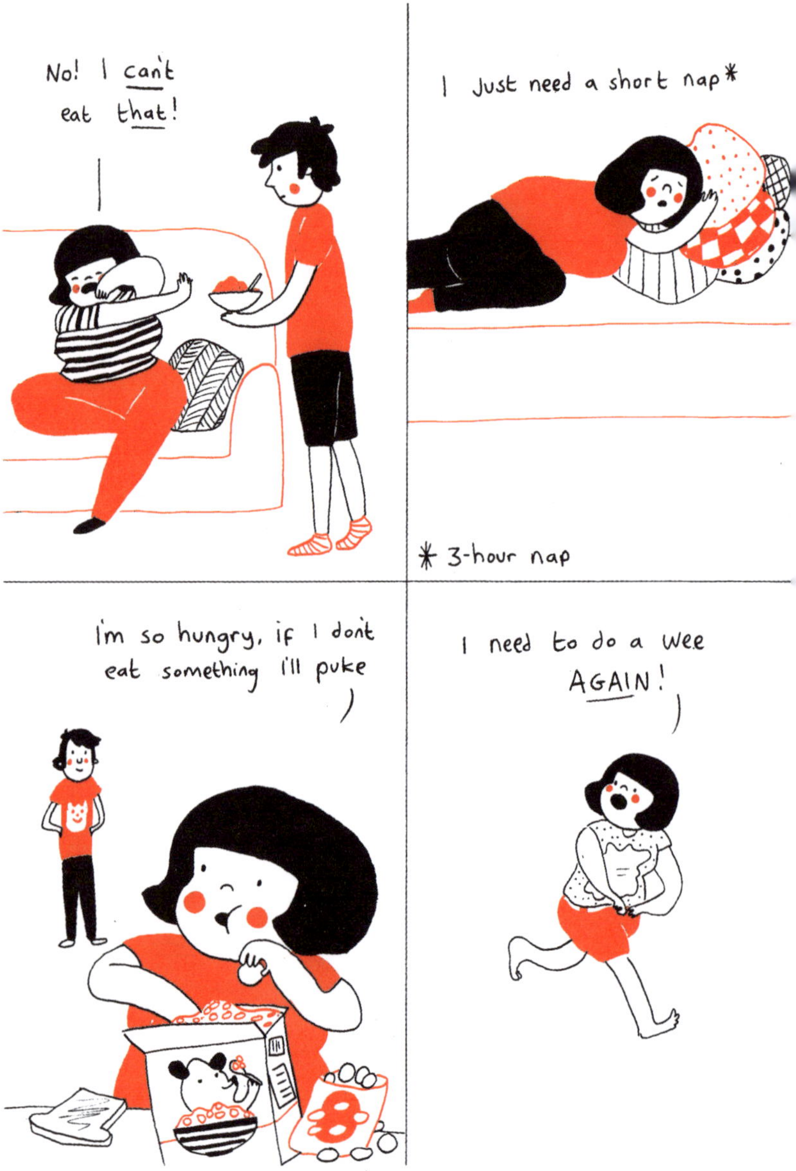
No! I can't eat that!
I just need a short nap*
* 3-hour nap
I'm so hungry, if I don't eat something I'll puke
I need to do a wee AGAIN!

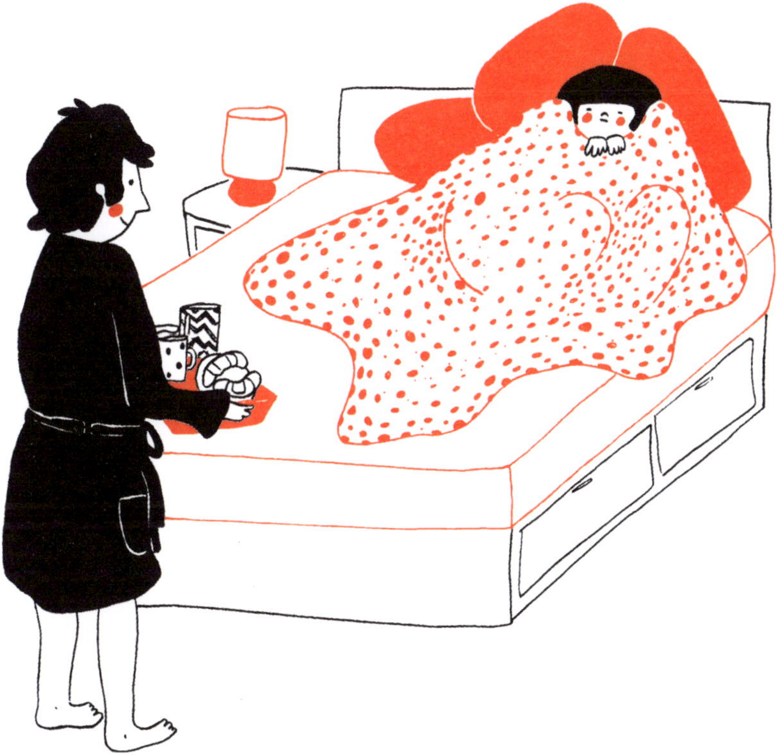

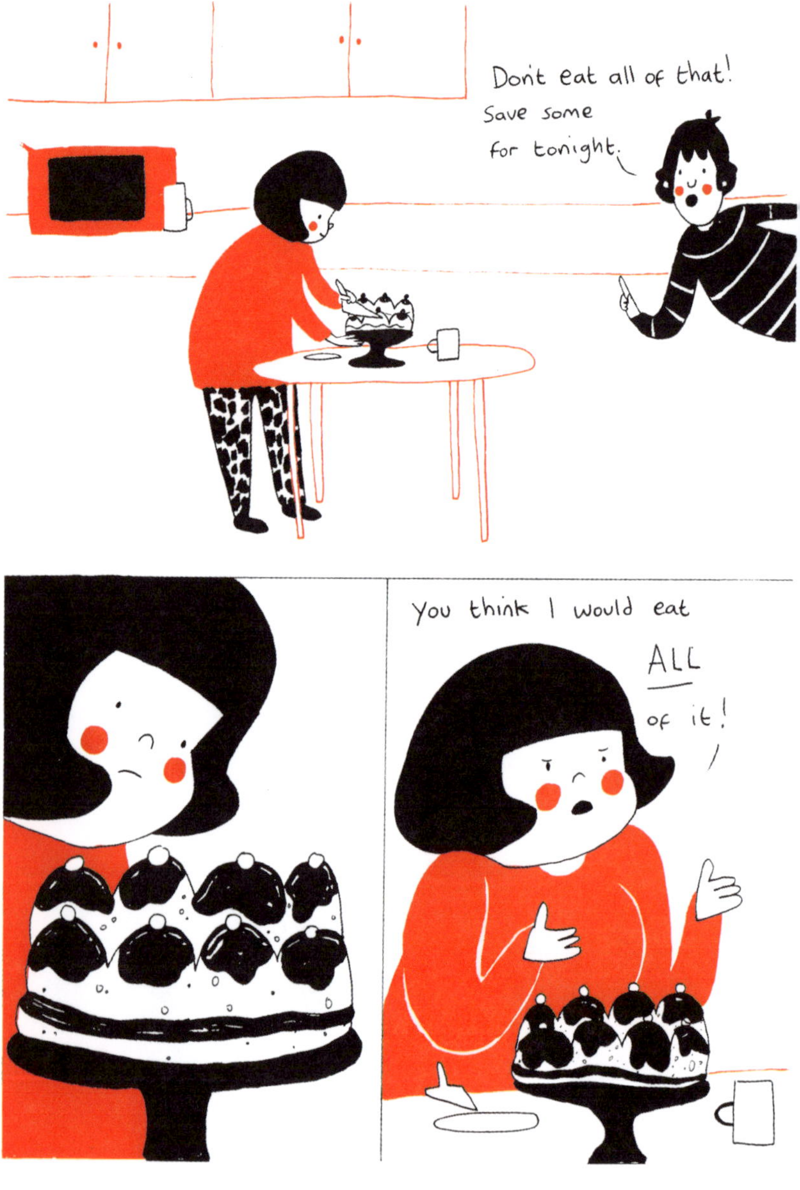
Don't eat all of that!
Save some for tonight.
You think I would eat ALL of it!

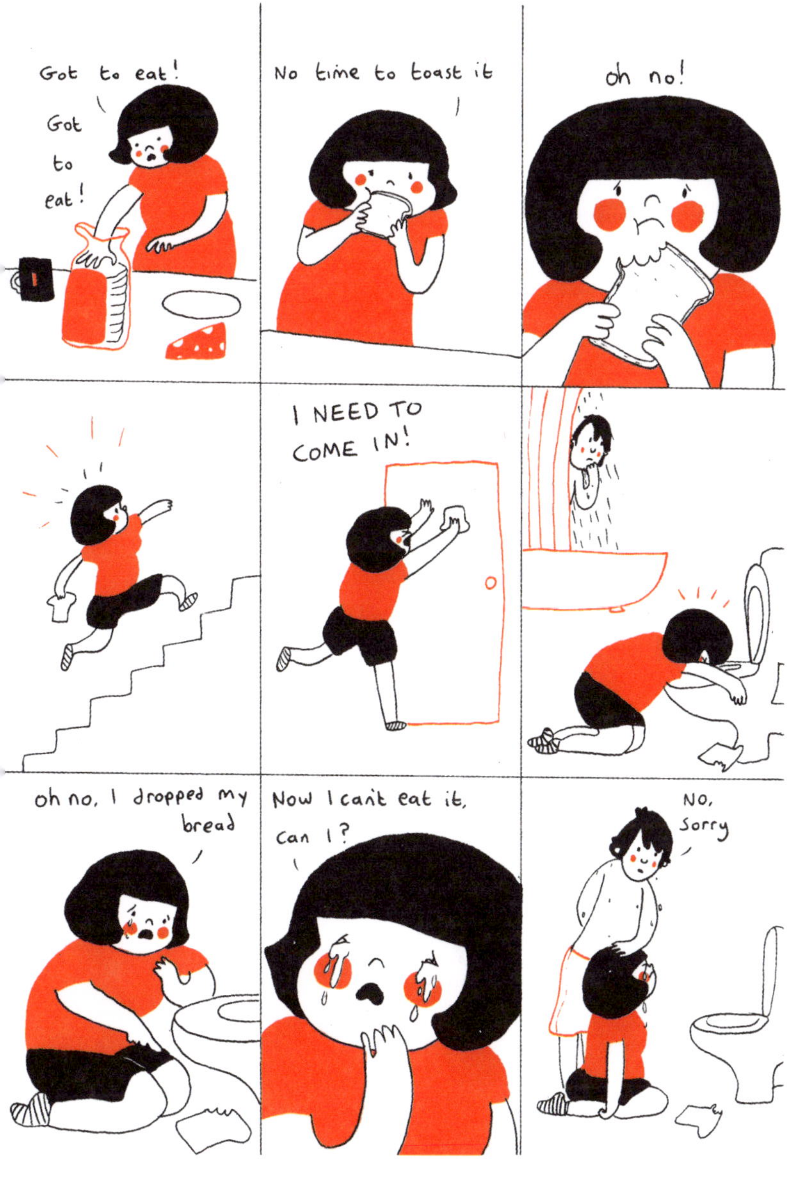
Got to eat!
Got to eat!
No time to toast it
oh no!
I NEED TO COME IN!
oh no, I dropped my bread
Now I can't eat it, can I?
No, sorry

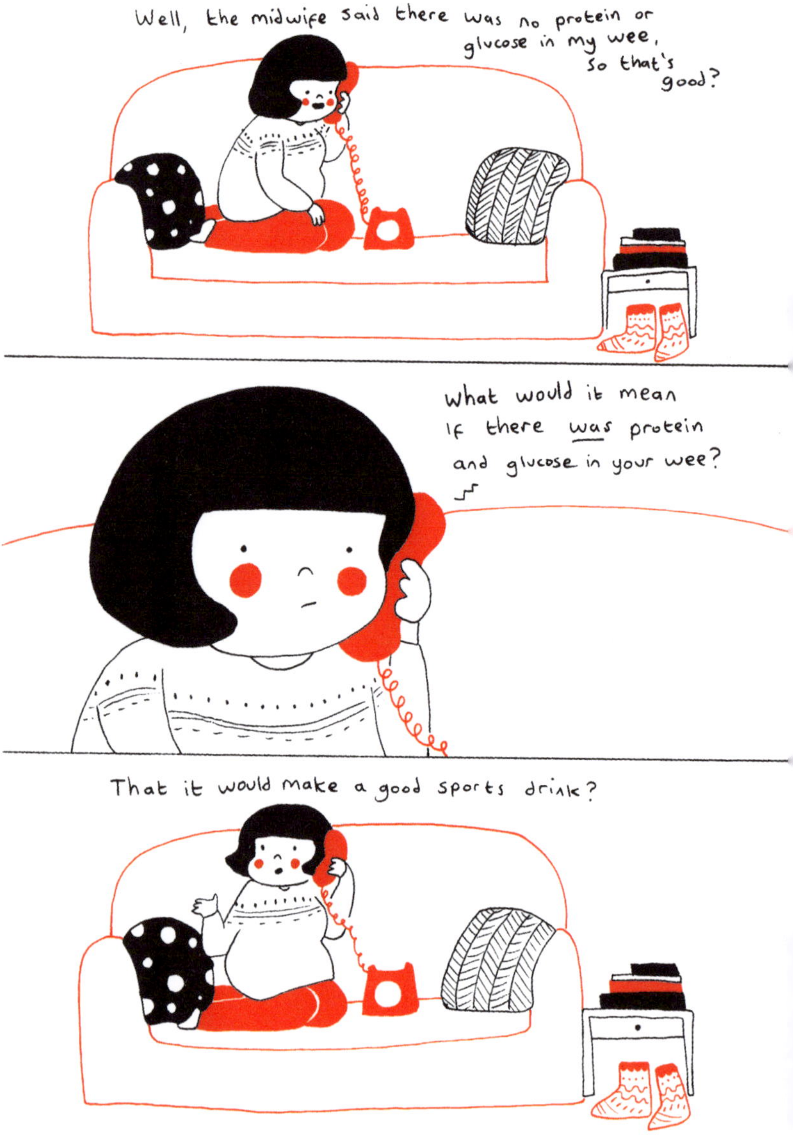
Well, the midwife said there was no protein or glucose in my wee, so that's good?
What would it mean if there was protein and glucose in your wee?
That it would make a good sports drink?

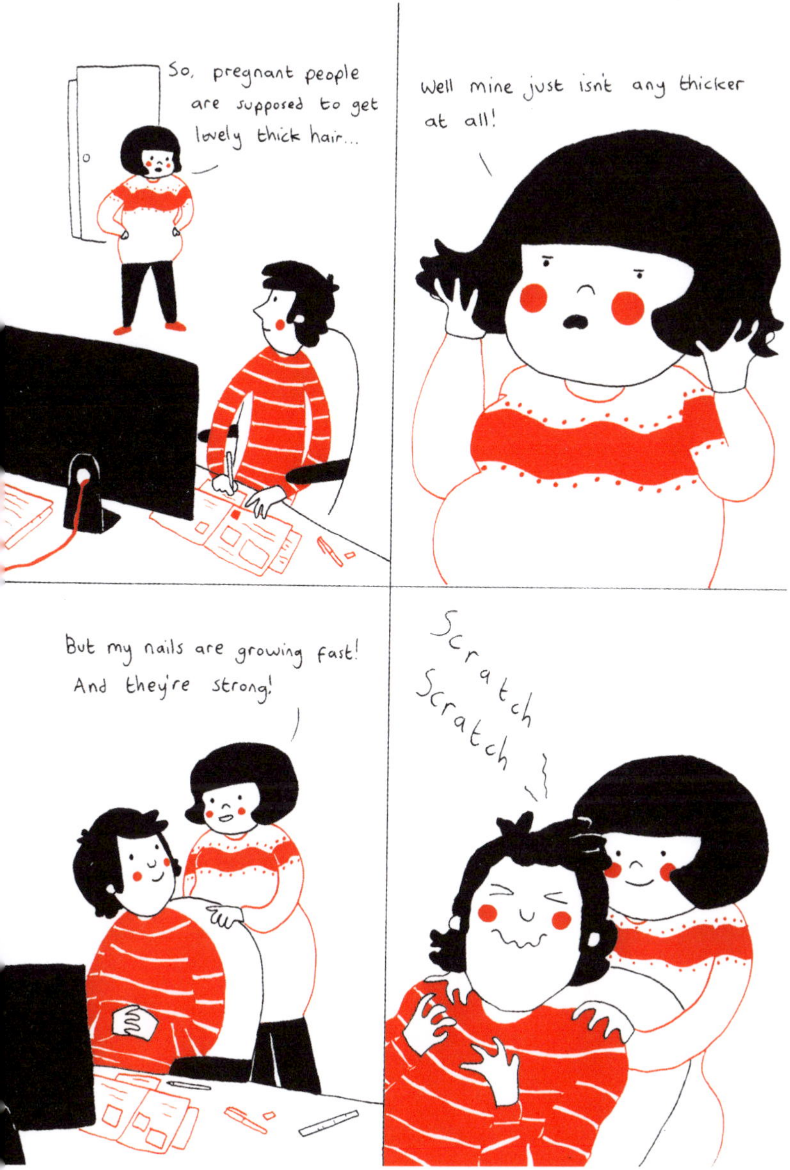
So, pregnant people are supposed to get lovely thick hair...
Well mine just isn't any thicker at all!
But my nails are growing fast! And they're strong!
Scratch Scratch

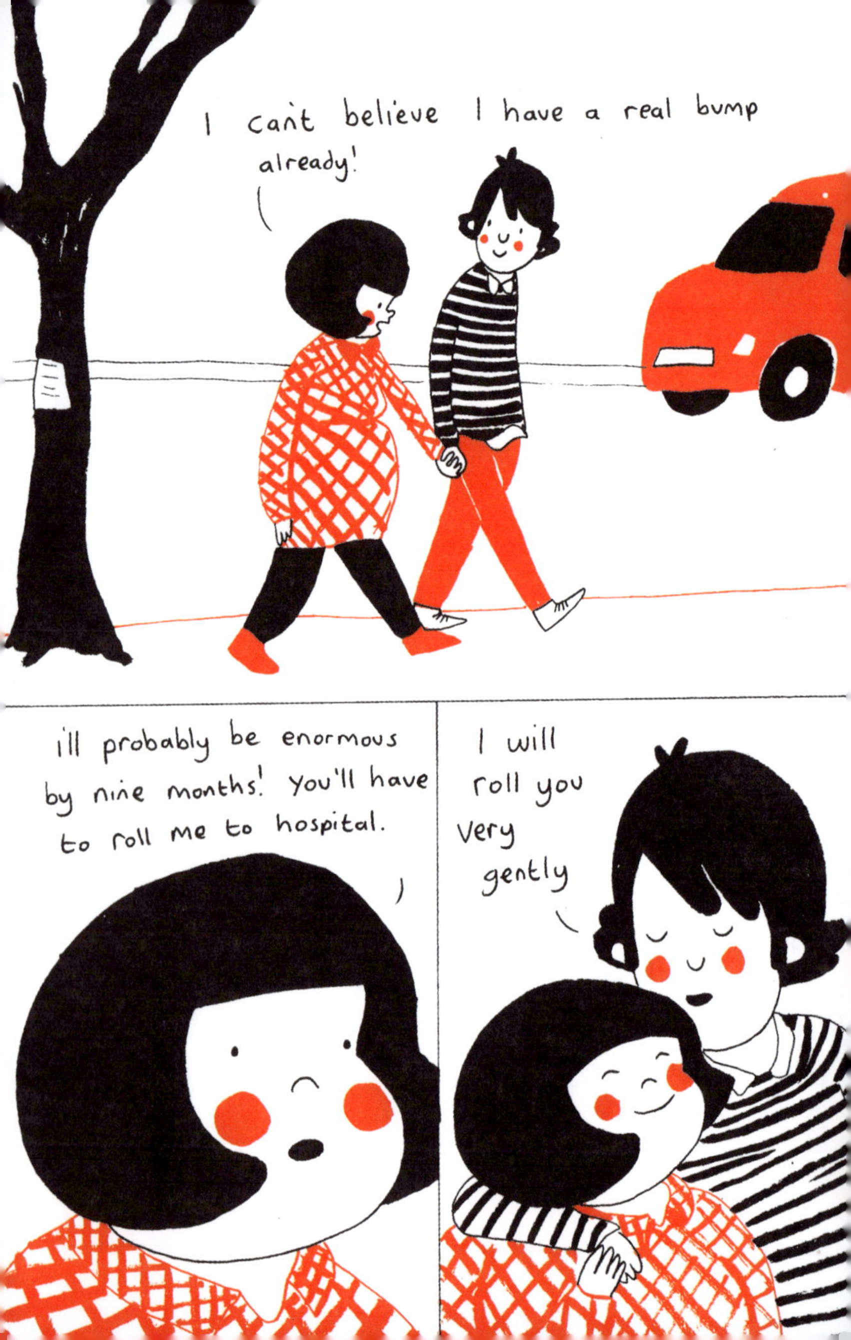
I can't believe I have a real bump already!
i'll probably be enormous by nine months! You'll have to roll me to hospital.
I will roll you very gently

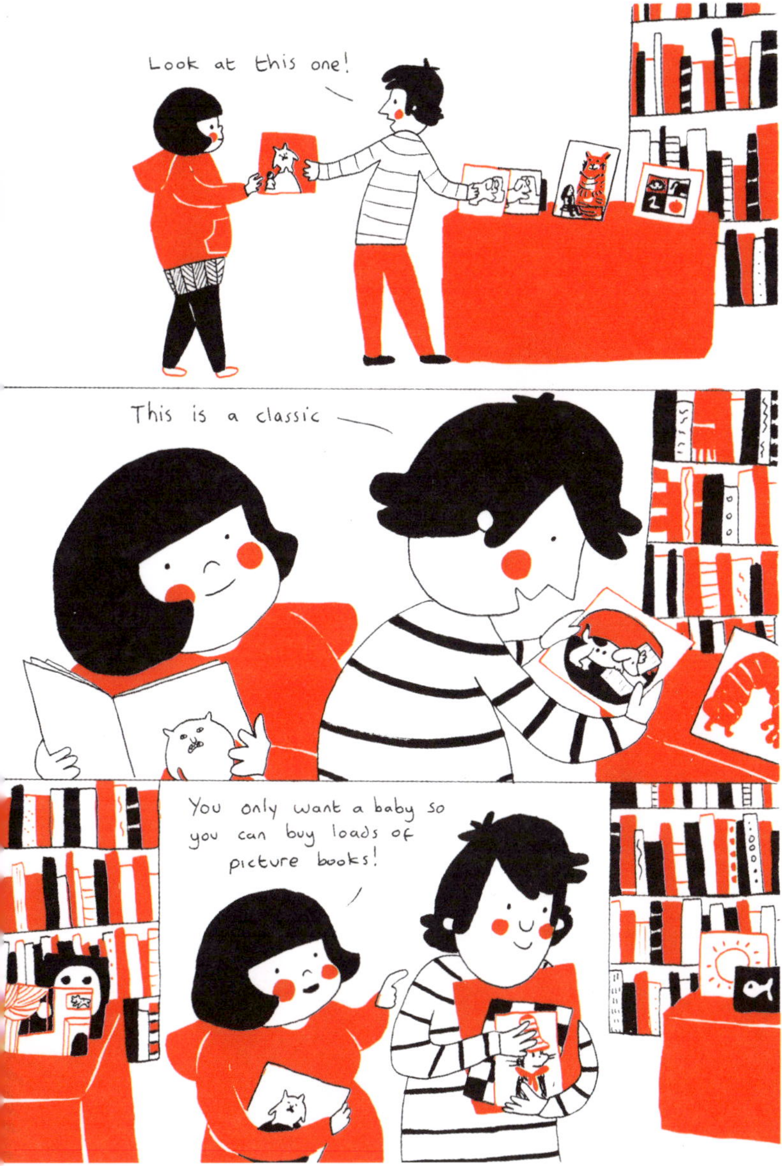
Look at this one!
This is a classic
You only want a baby so you can buy loads of picture books!

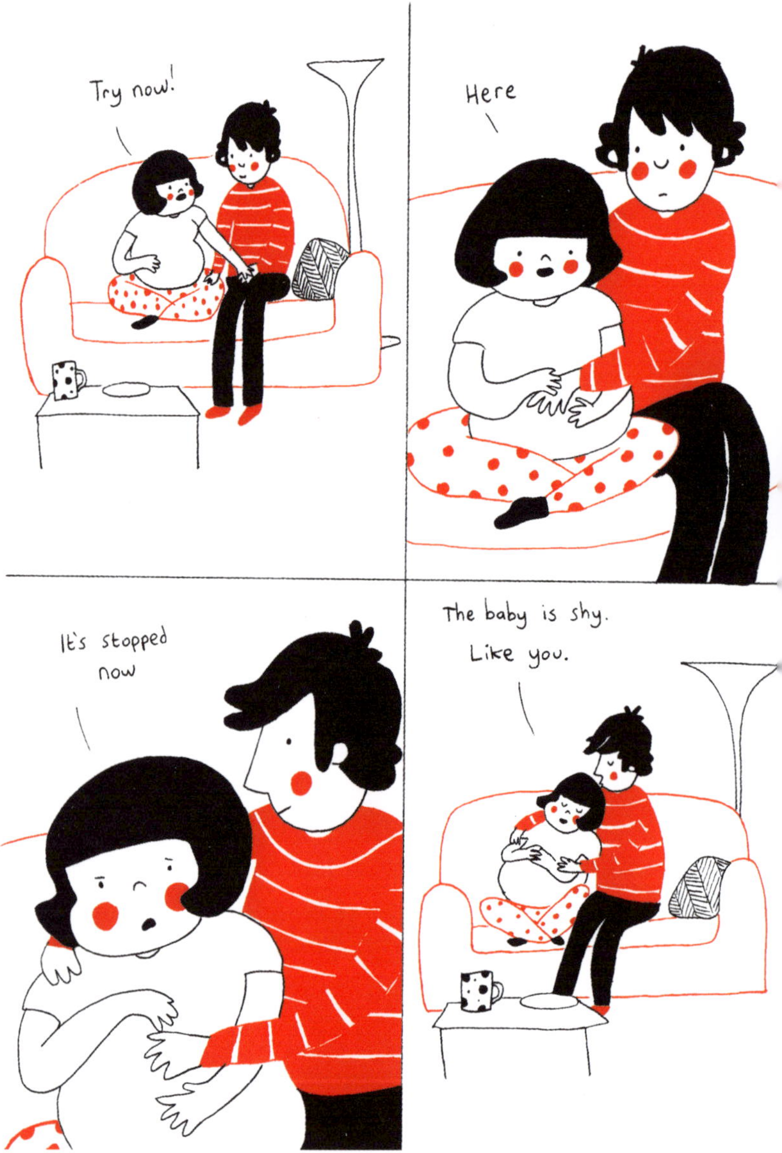

Try now!
Here
It's stopped now
The baby is shy.
Like you.

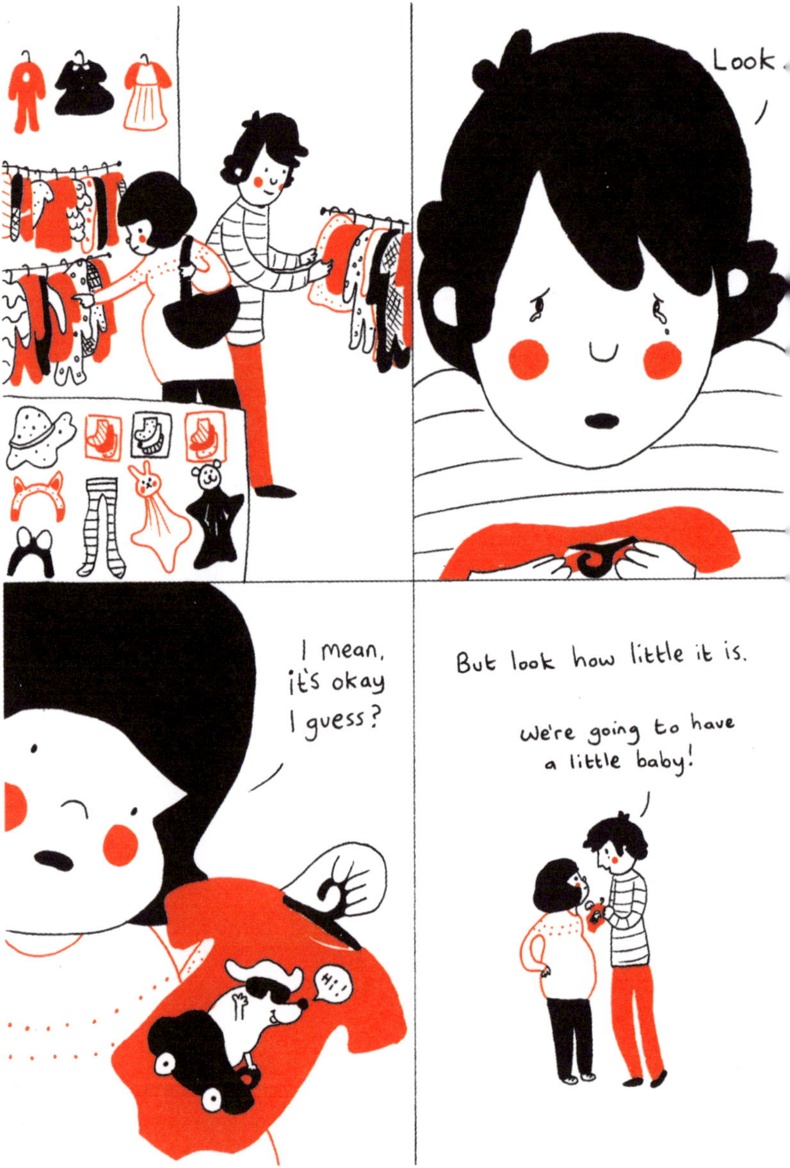
Look.
I mean, it's okay I guess?
Hi!
But look how little it is.
We're going to have a little baby!

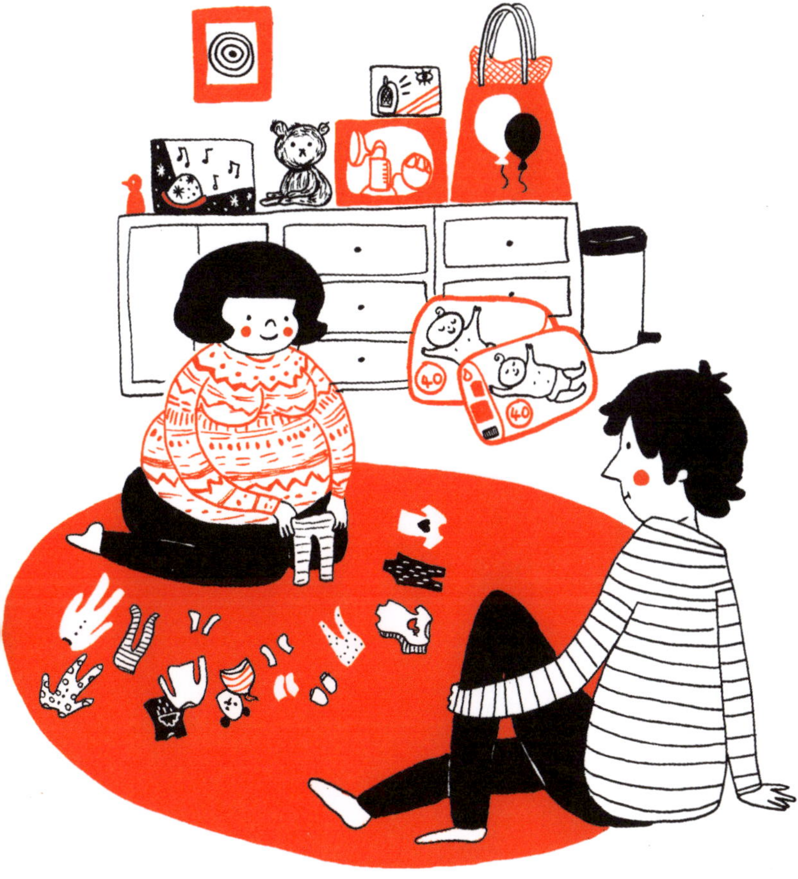

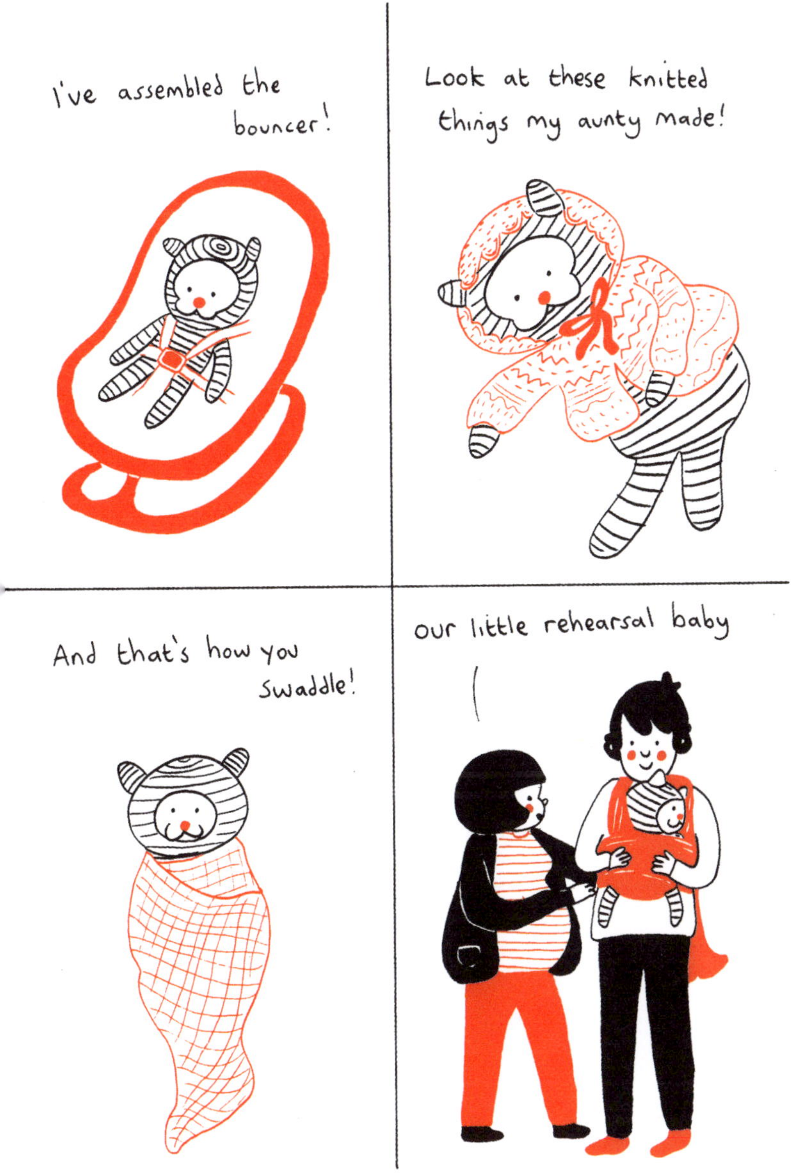
I've assembled the bouncer!
Look at these knitted things my aunty made!
And that's how you swaddle!
our little rehearsal baby

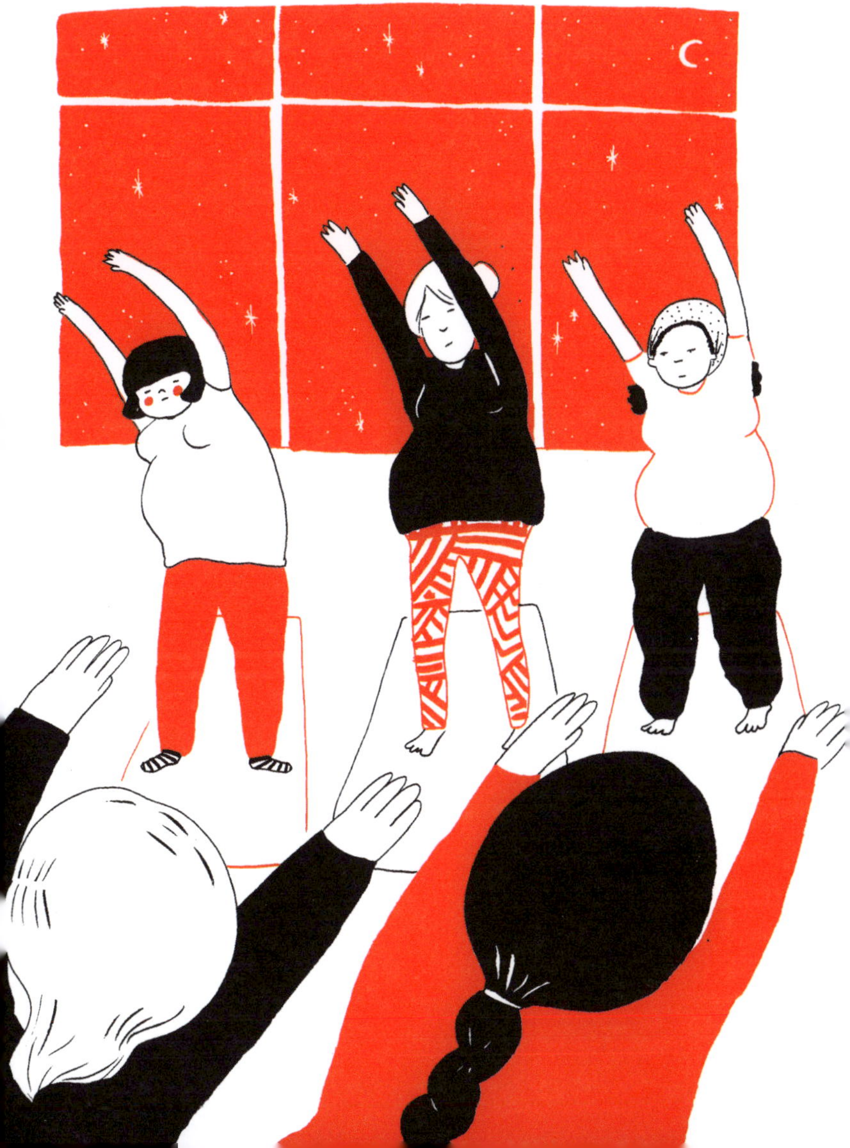

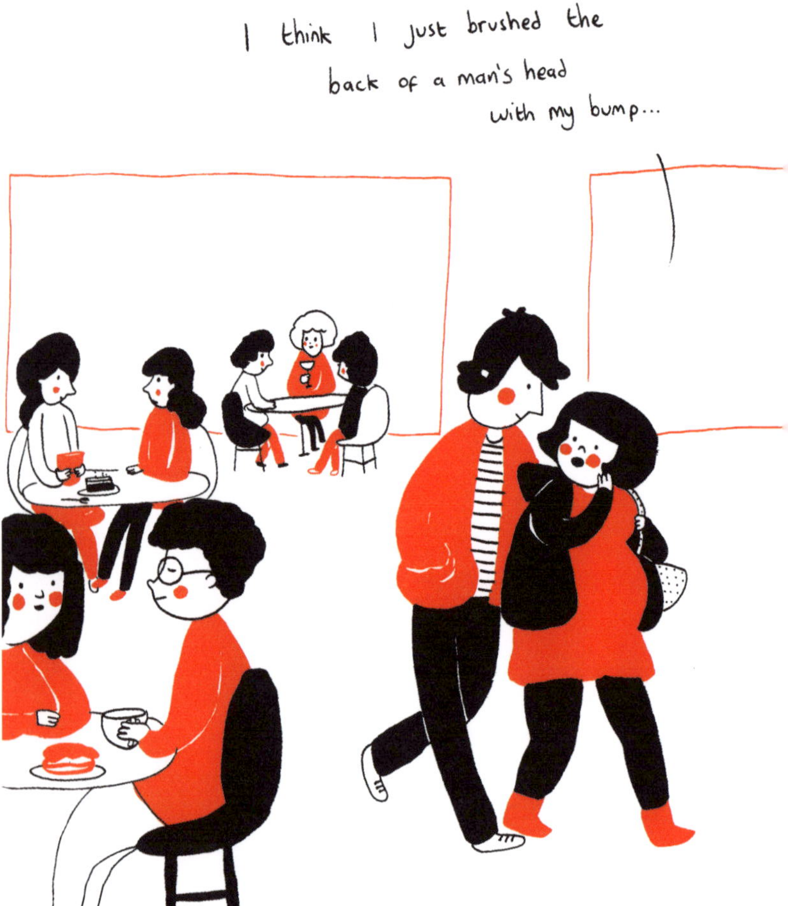
I think I just brushed the back of a man's head with my bump...

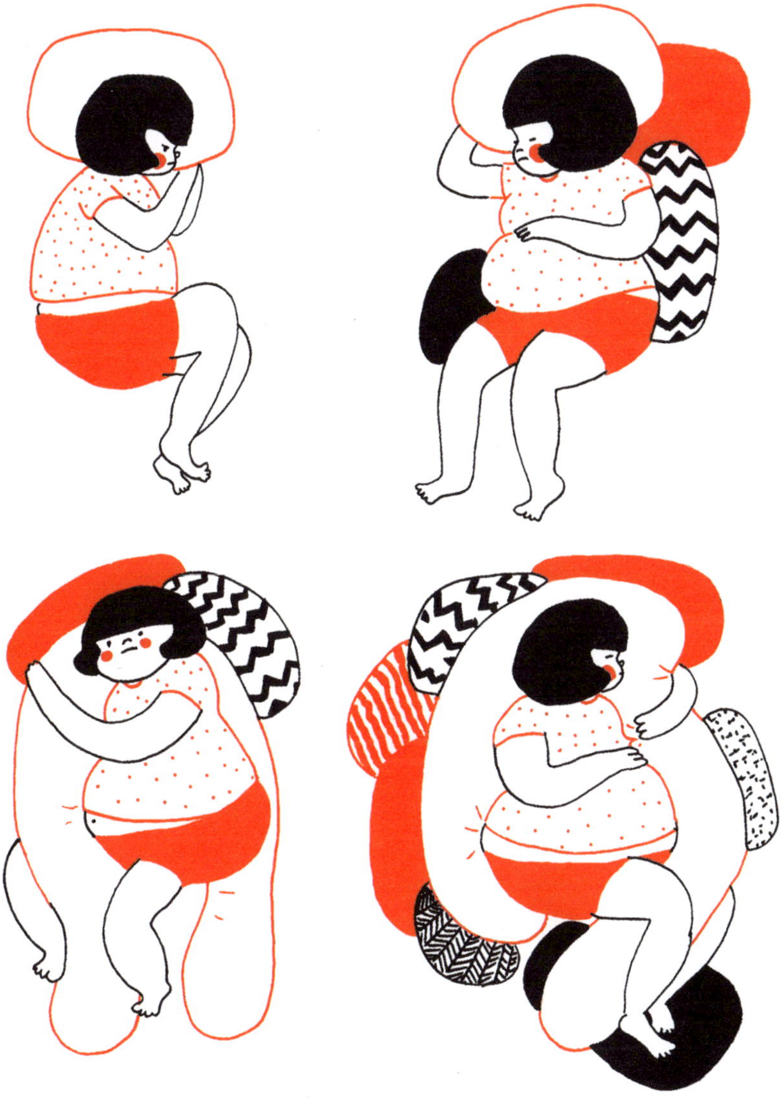

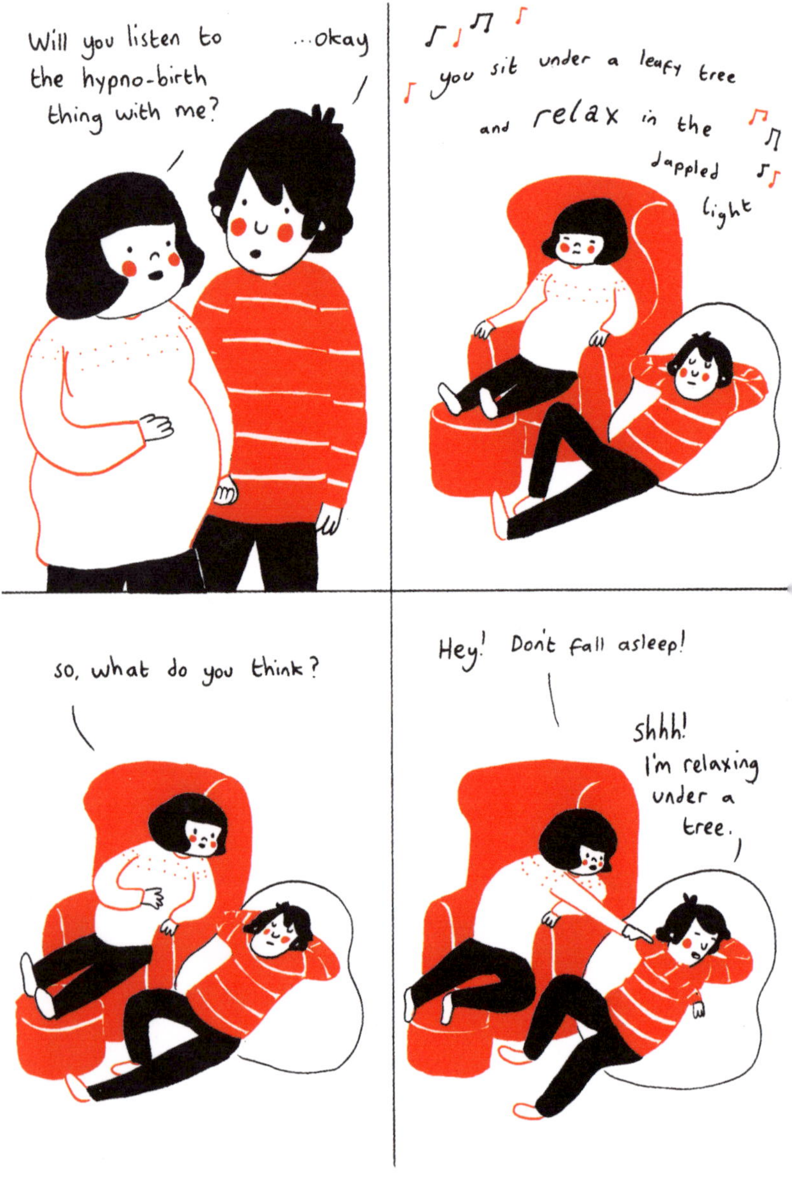
Will you listen to the hypno-birth thing with me?
...okay
you sit under a leafy tree and relax in the dappled light
so, what do you think?
Hey! Don't fall asleep!
shhh! I'm relaxing under a tree.

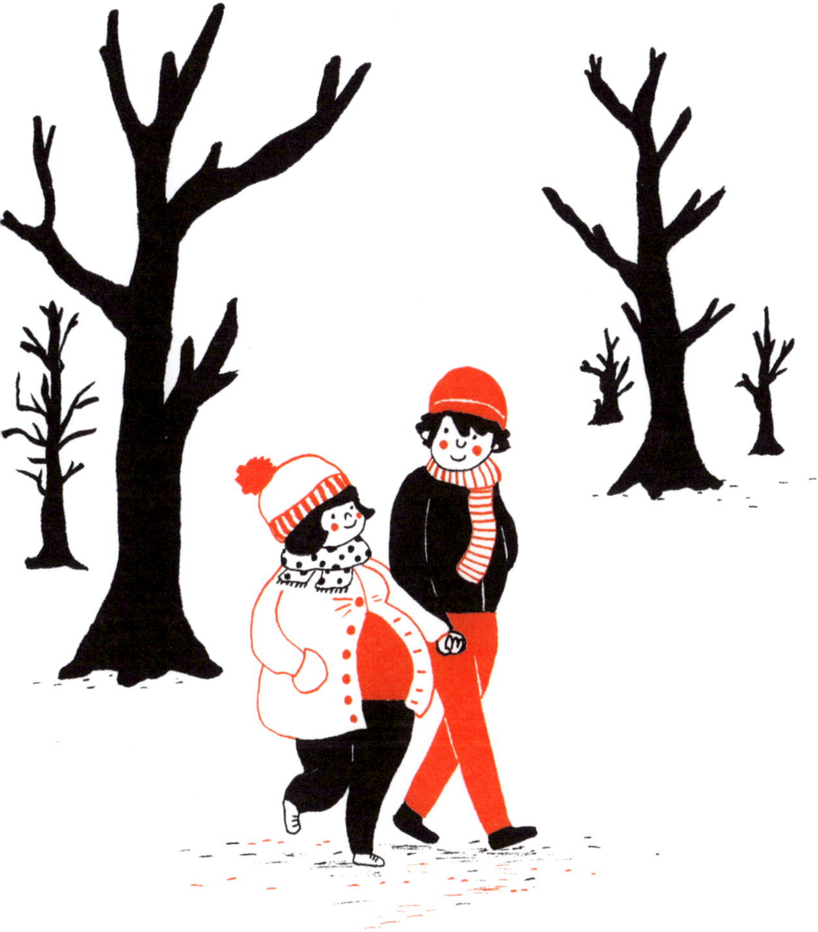

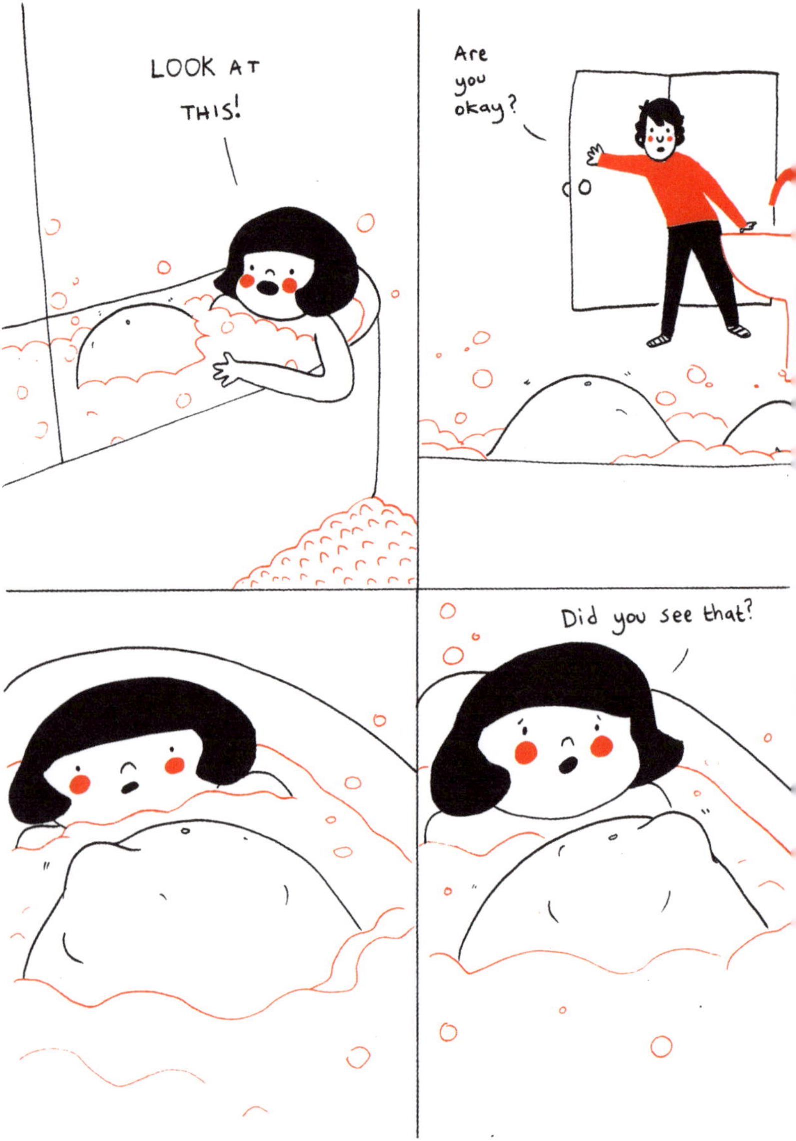
LOOK AT THIS!
Are you okay?
Did you see that?

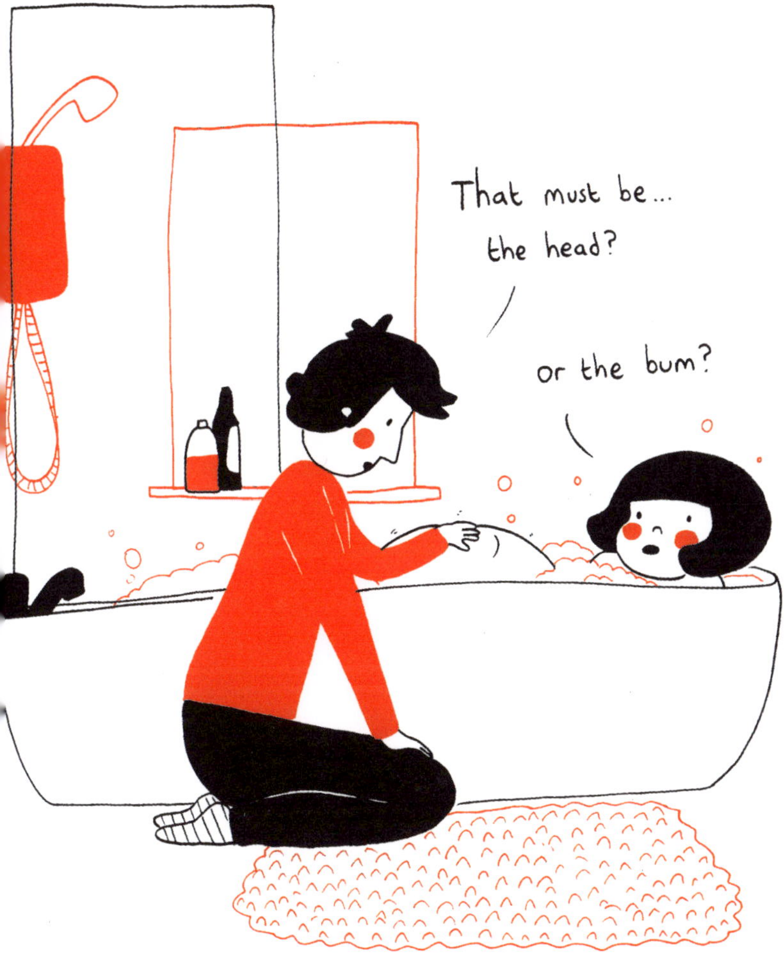
That must be...
the head?
or the bum?

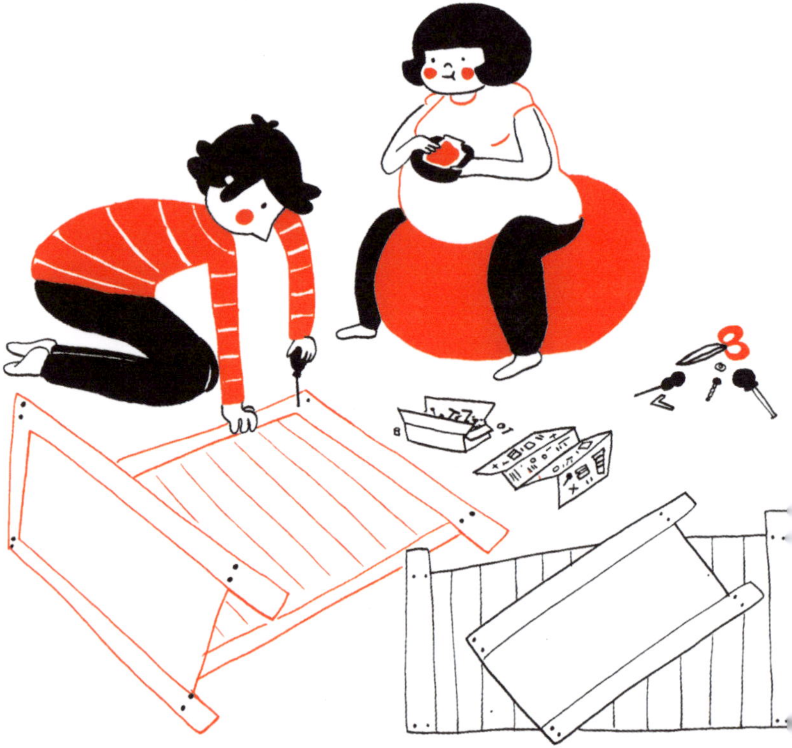

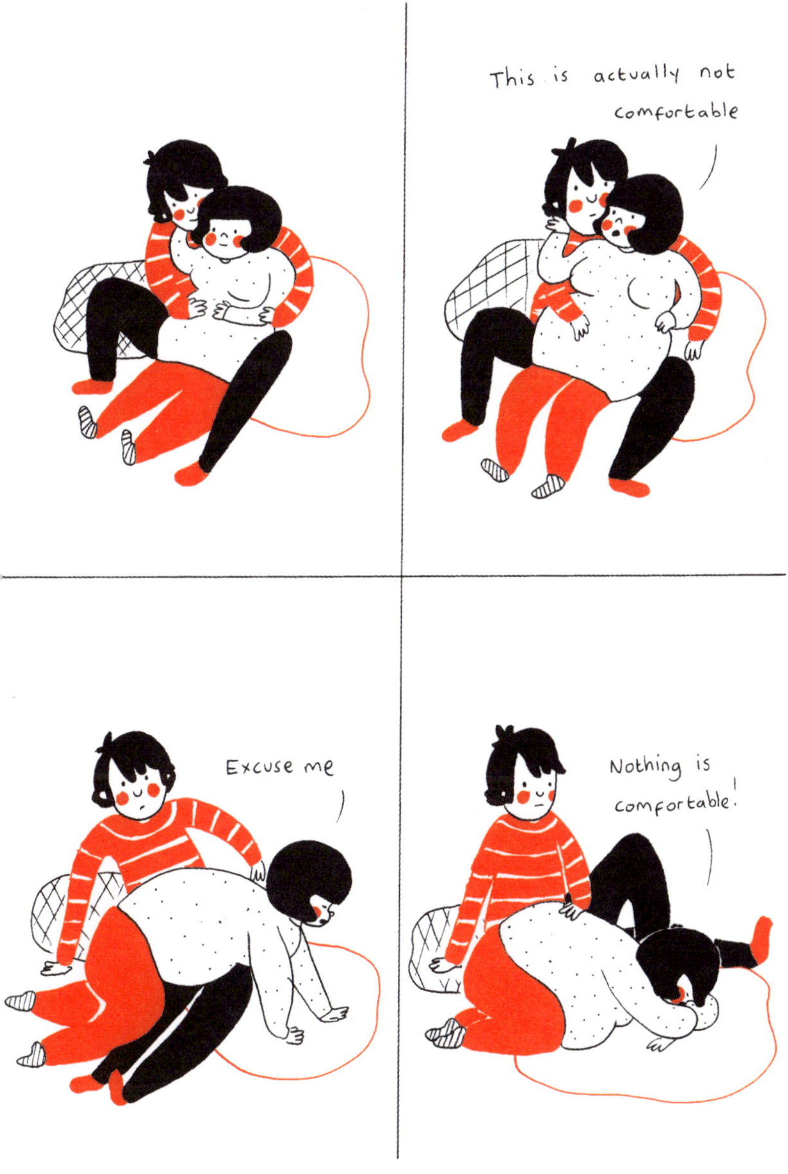
This is actually not comfortable
Excuse me
Nothing is comfortable!

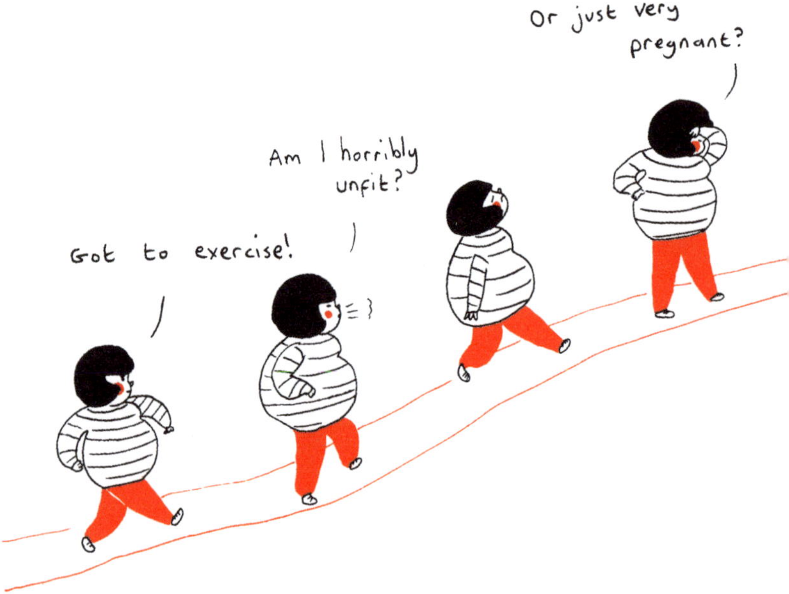
Got to exercise!
Am I horribly unfit?
Or just very pregnant?

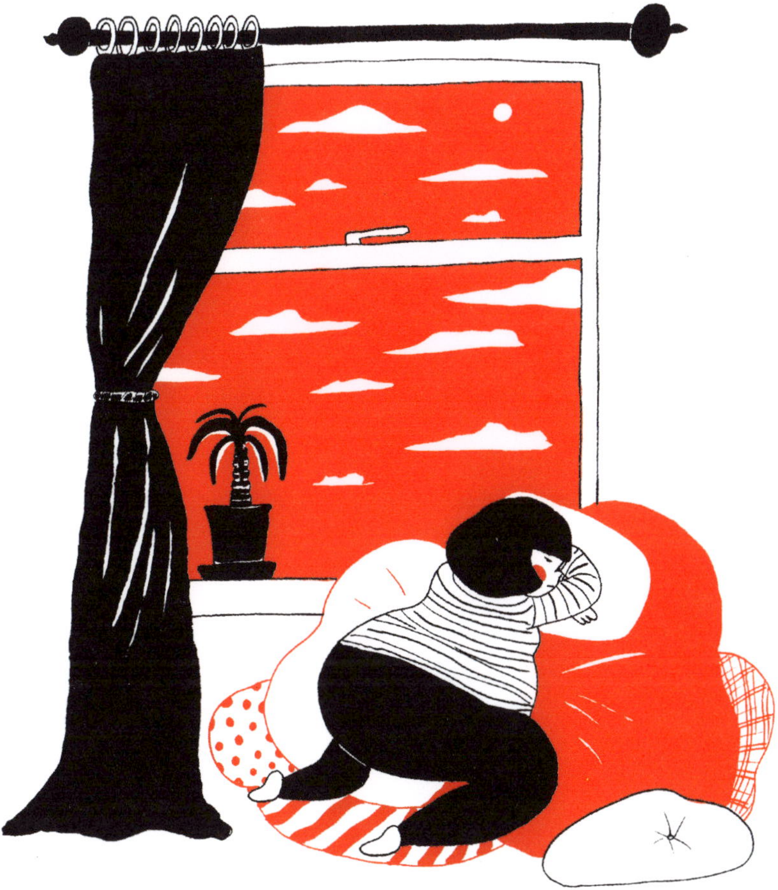

Thank you for coming to my appointment with me. You didn't have to.

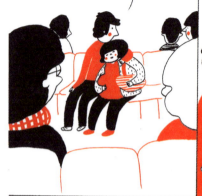

I think they just want to give me some iron tablets. I have low platelets apparently.

The doctor recommends that we induce labor today

TODAY?!

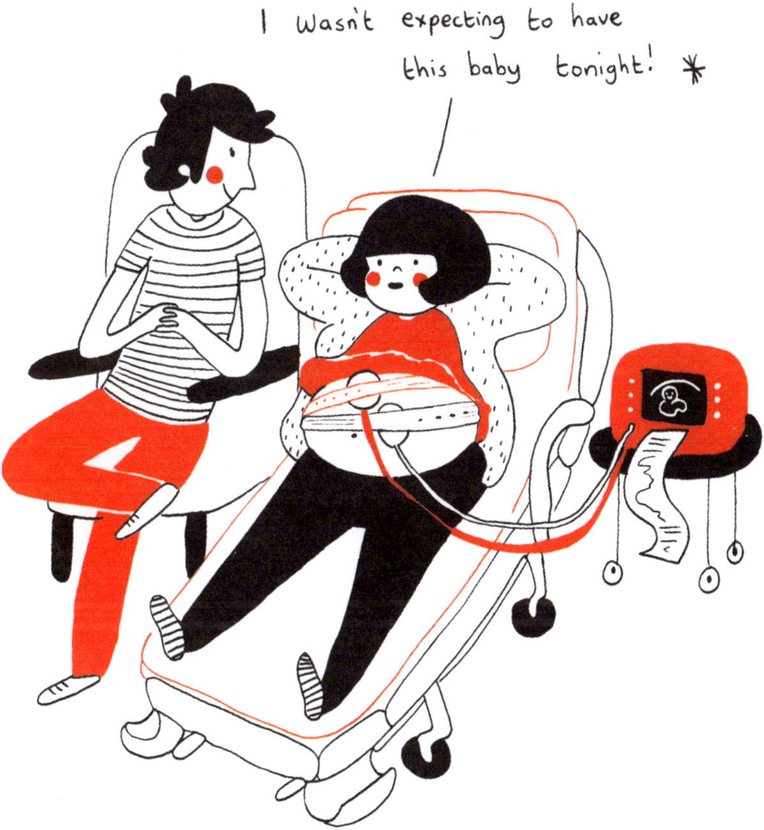
I wasn't expecting to have this baby tonight! *

* In fact, it took two more days...

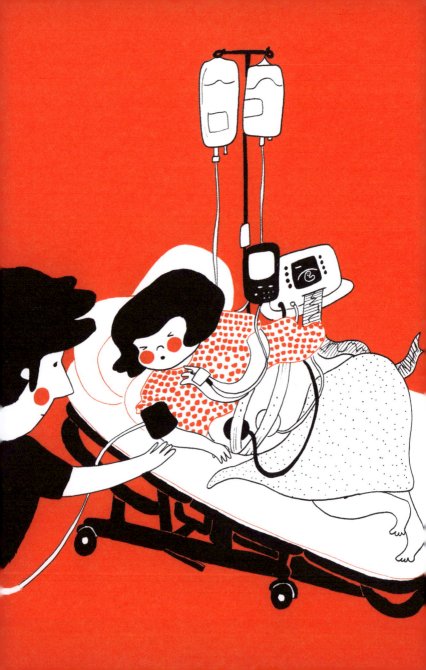

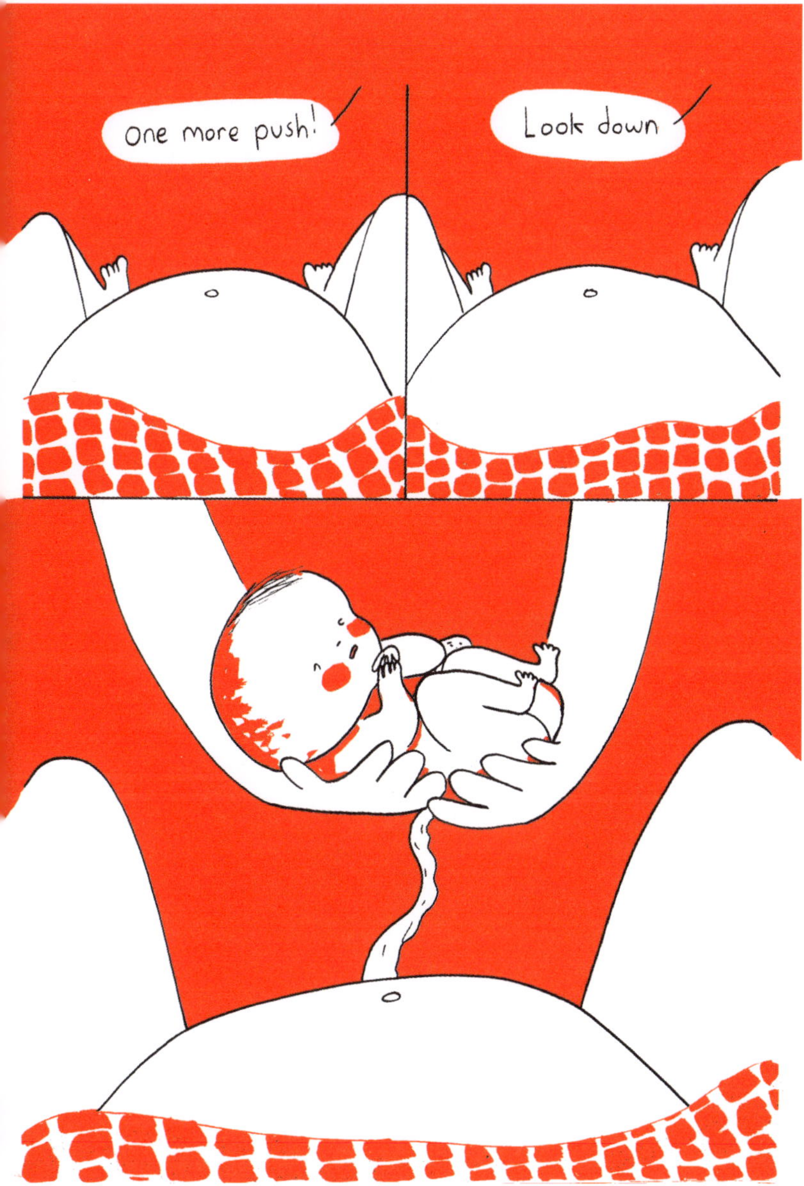
One more push!
Look down

Hello

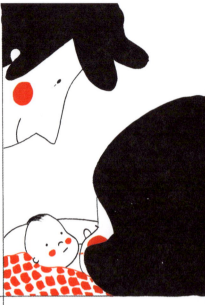

The way she's moving and squirming...

...feels the same as when she was inside!

44

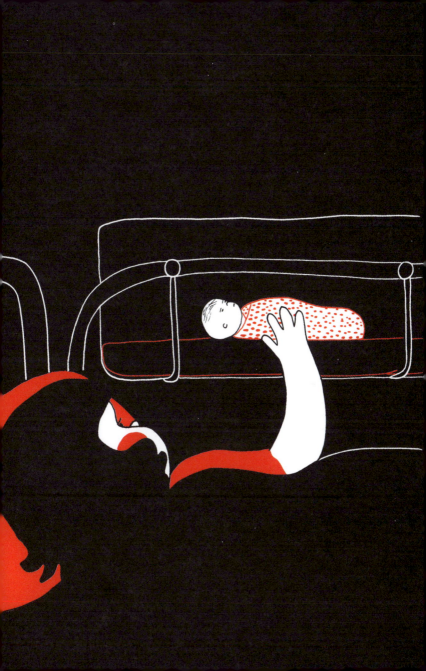

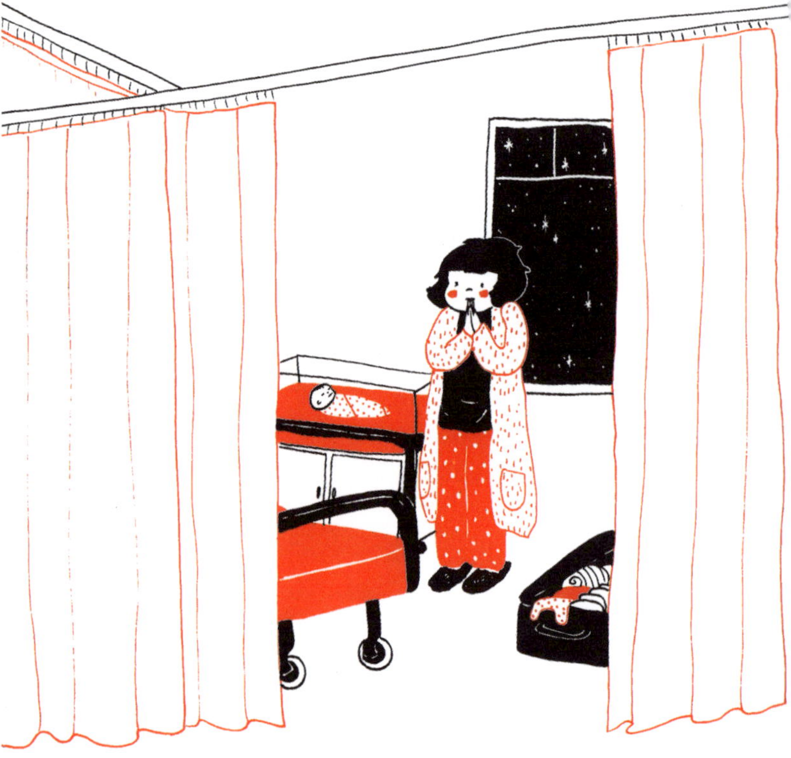

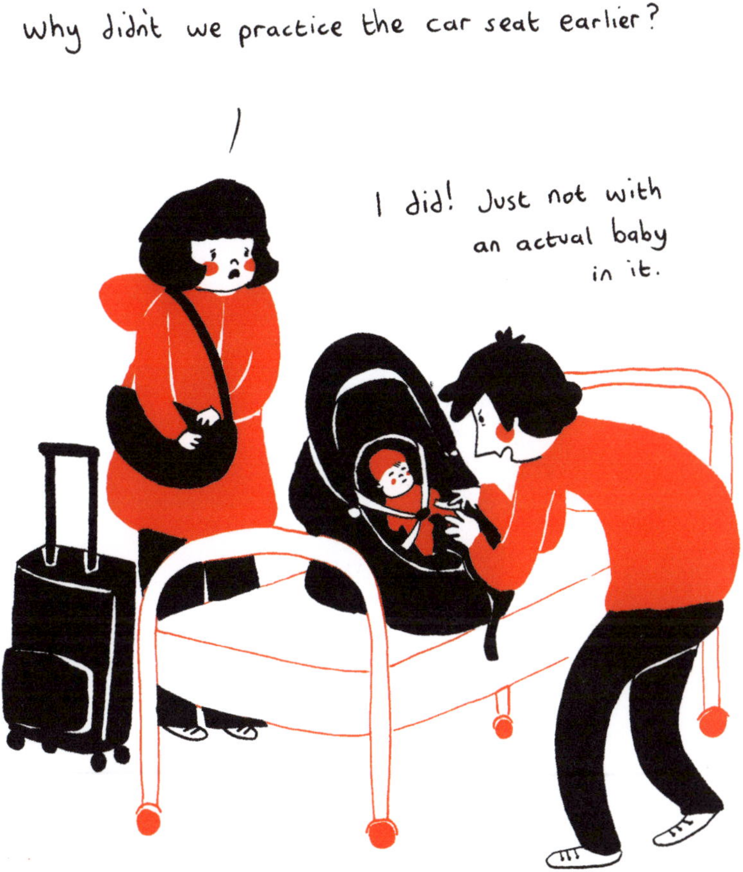
Why didn't we practice the car seat earlier?
I did! Just not with an actual baby in it.

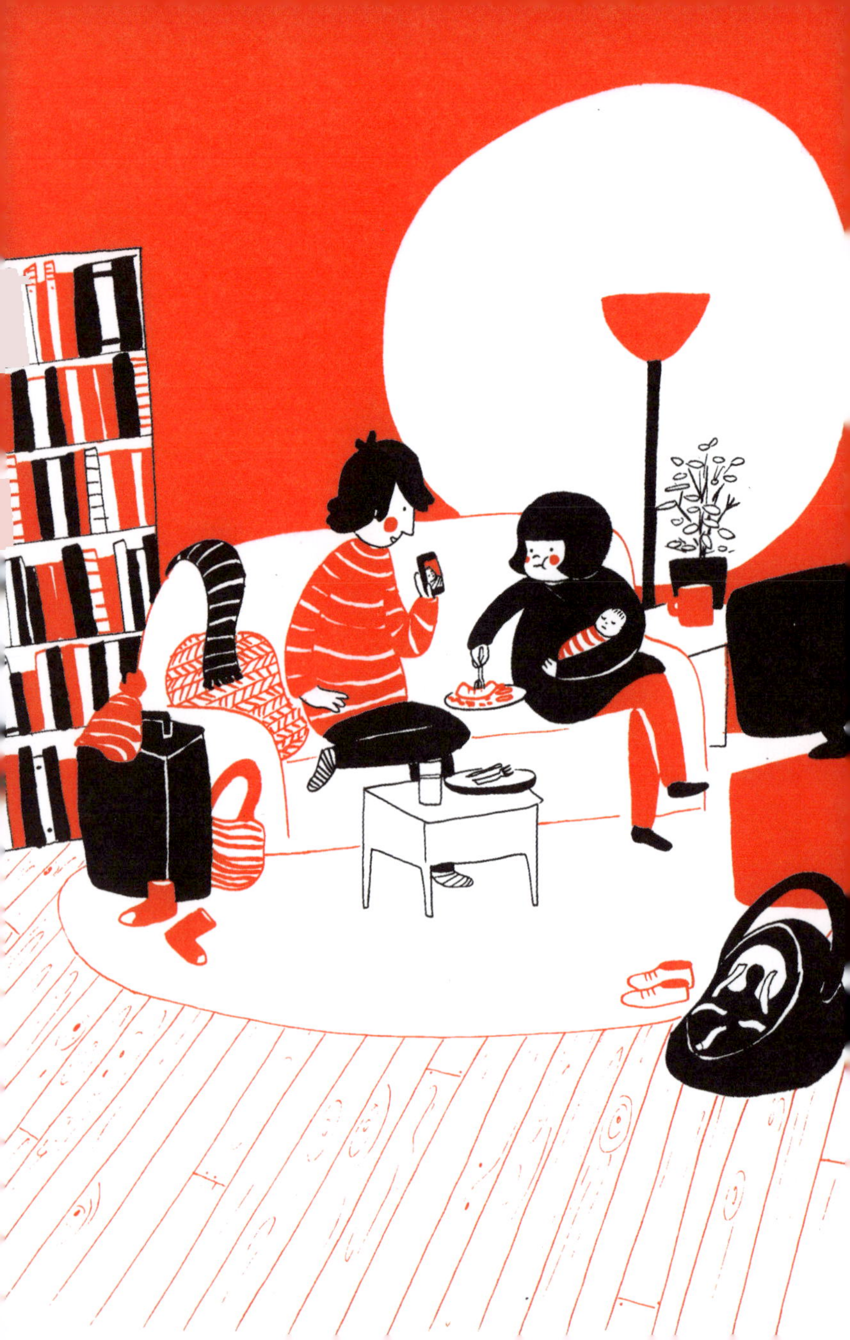

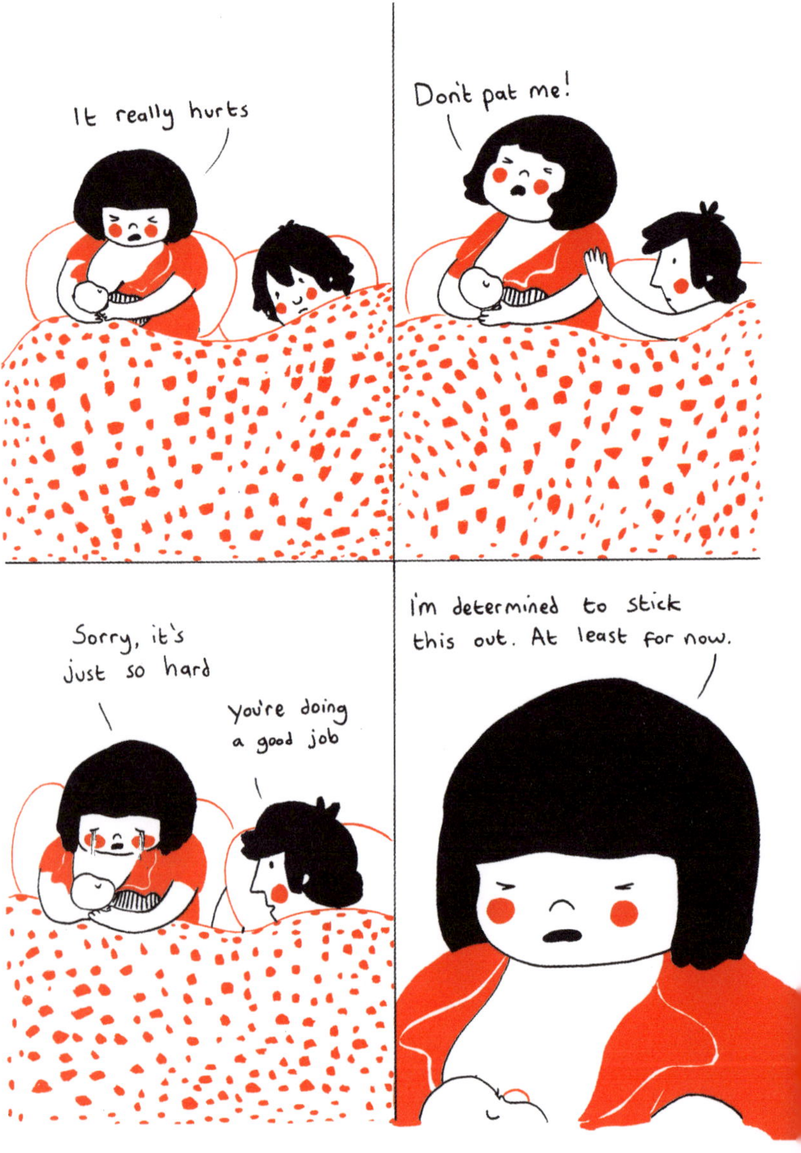
It really hurts
Don't pat me!
Sorry, it's just so hard
You're doing a good job
I'm determined to stick this out. At least for now.

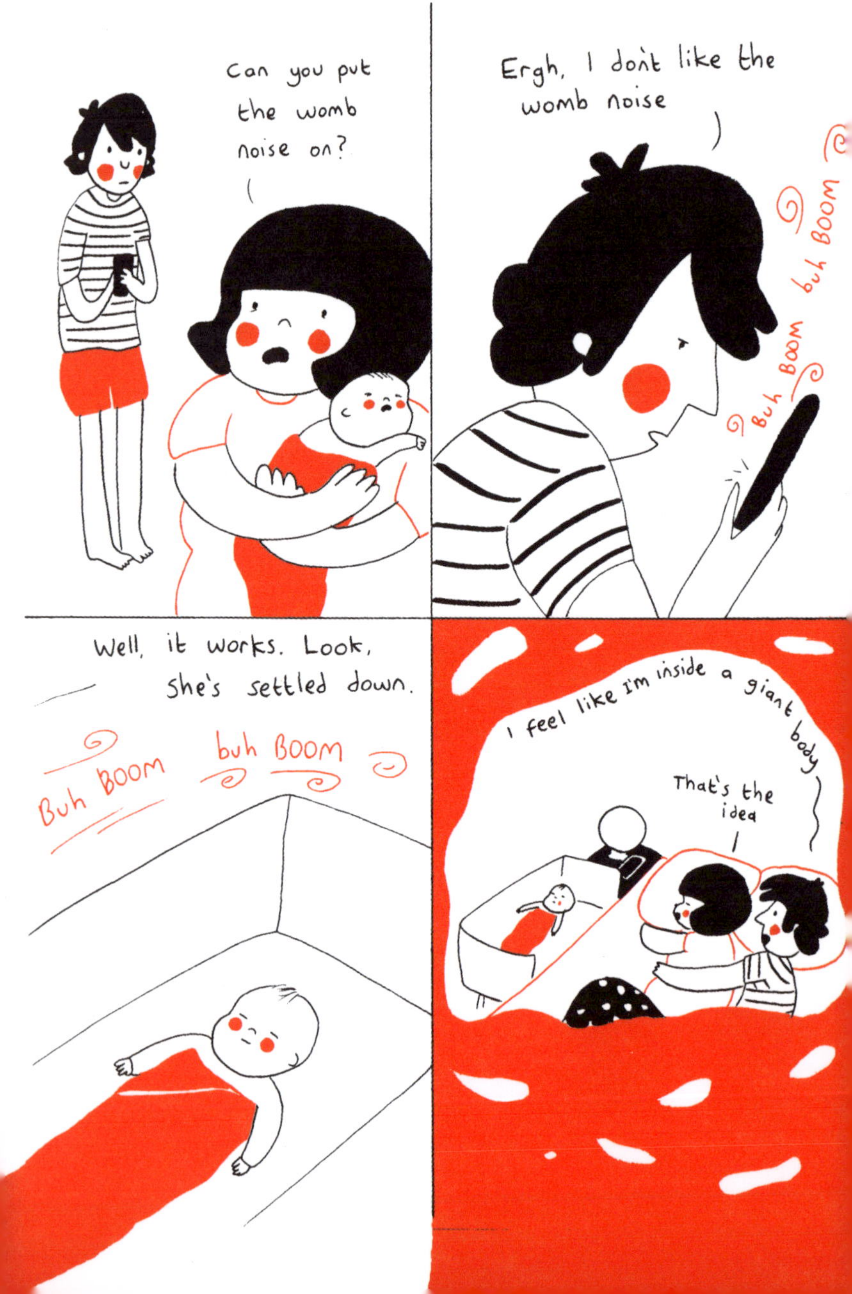
Can you put the womb noise on?
Ergh, I don't like the womb noise
Buh BOOM buh BOOM
Well, it works. Look, she's settled down.
Buh BOOM buh BOOM
I feel like I'm inside a giant body
That's the idea

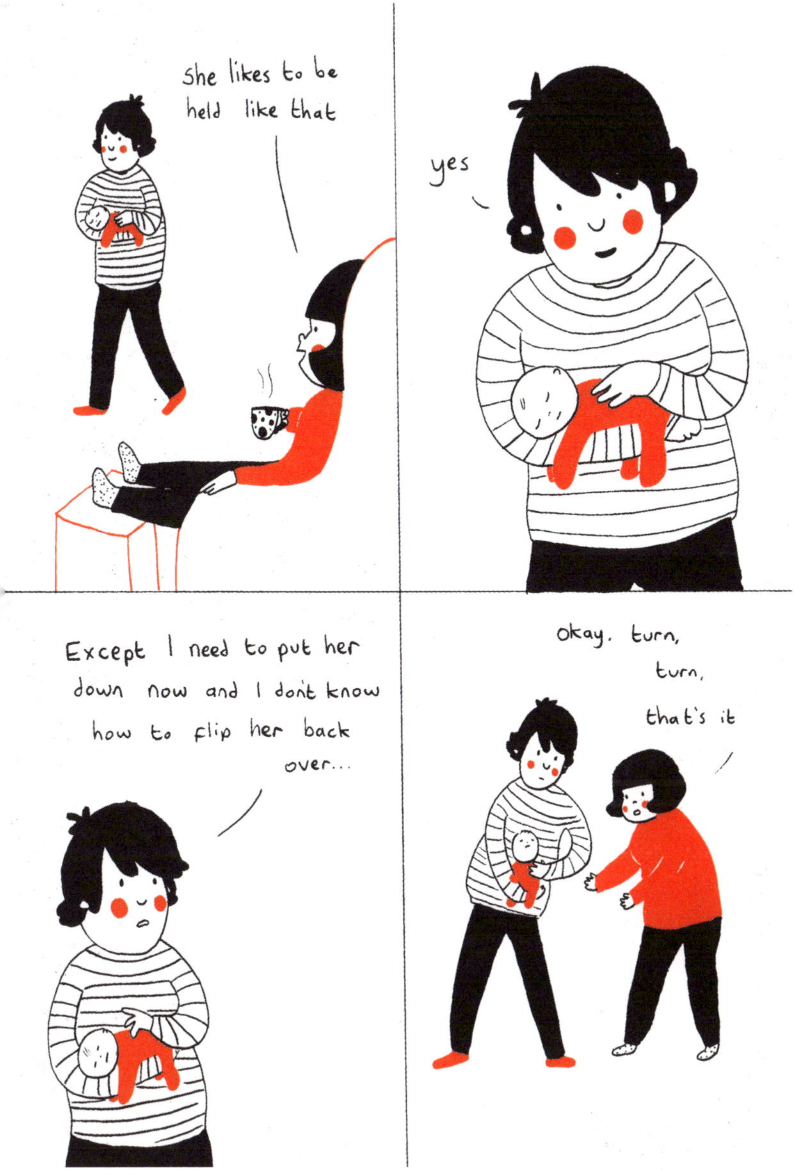
She likes to be held like that
yes
Except I need to put her down now and I don't know how to flip her back over...
okay. turn,
turn,
that's it

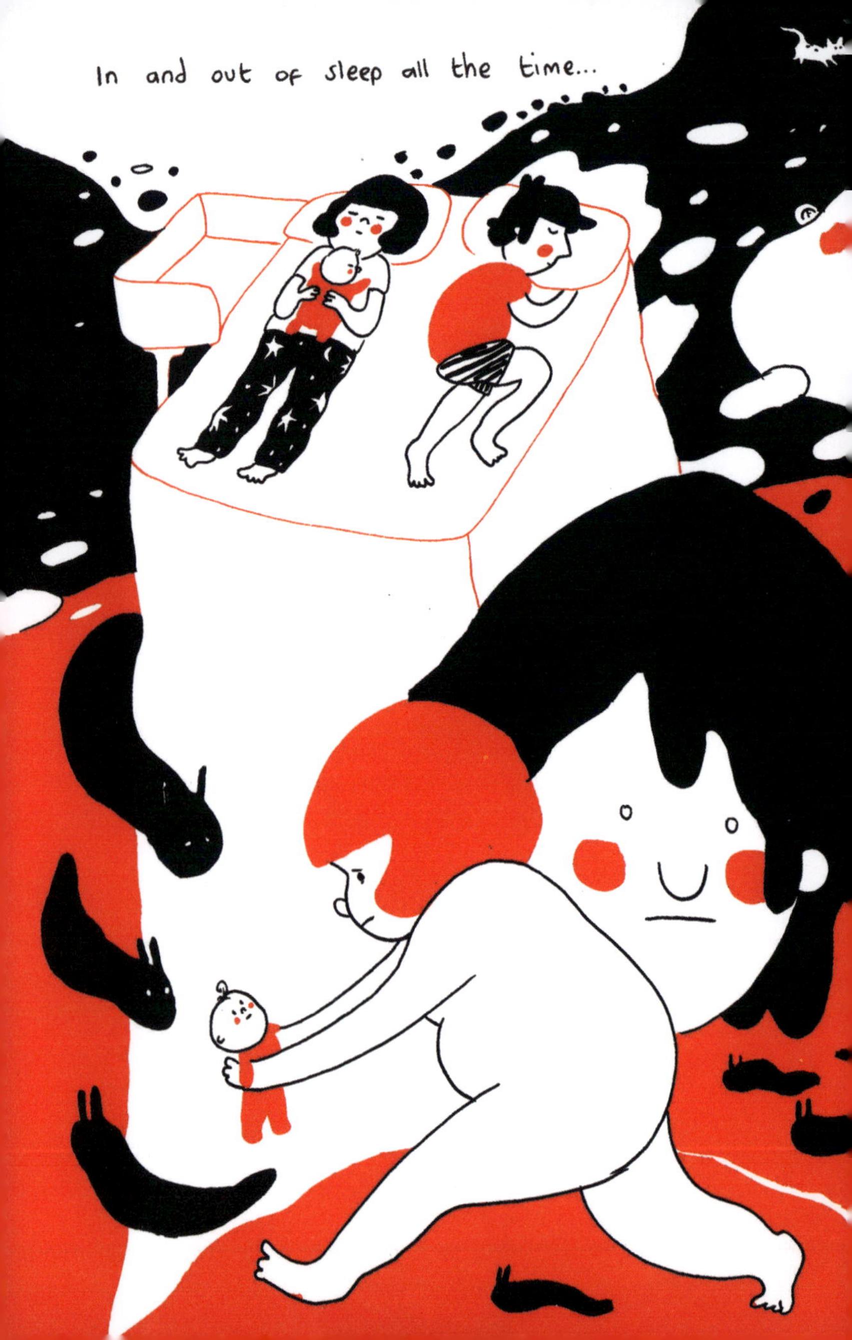
In and out of sleep all the time...

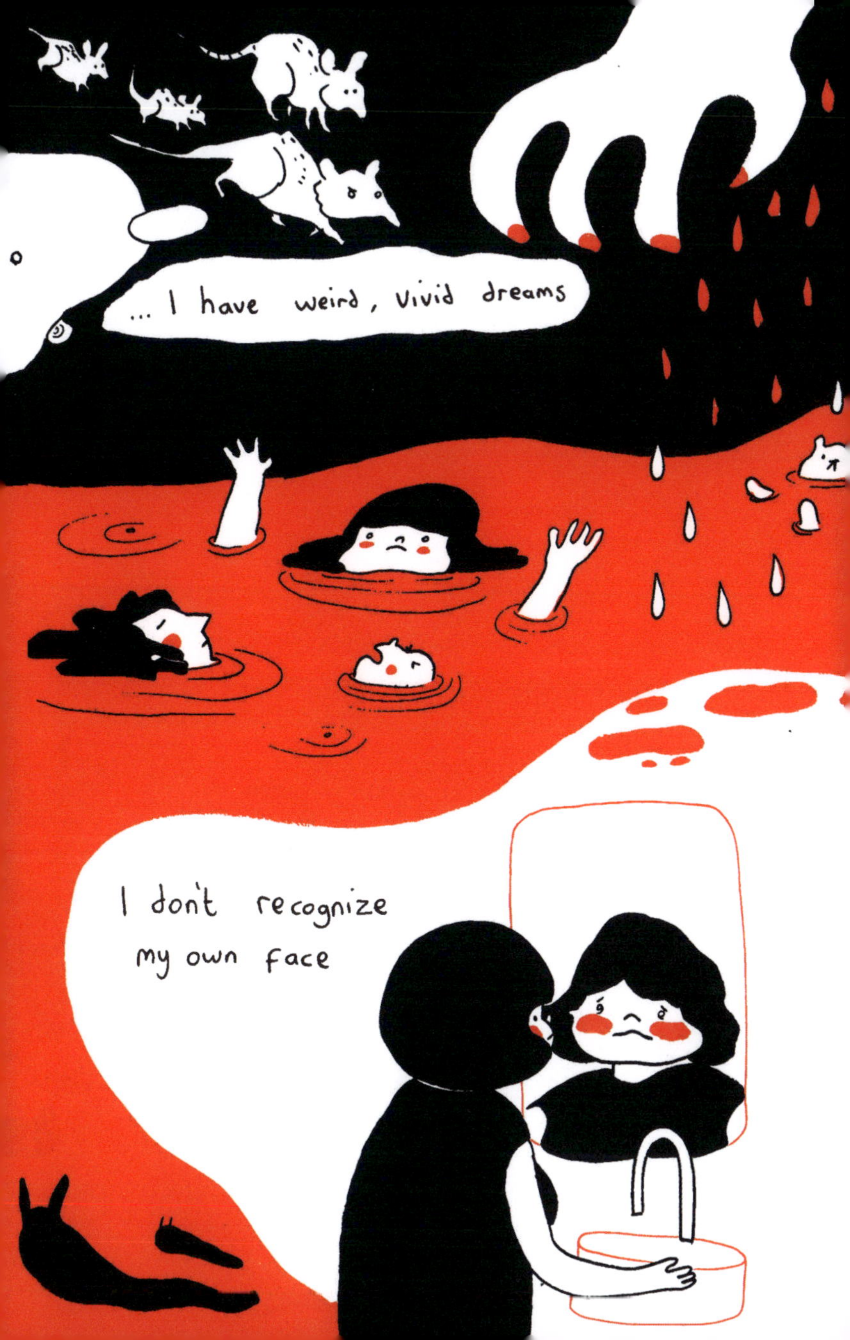
... I have weird, vivid dreams
I don't recognize my own face

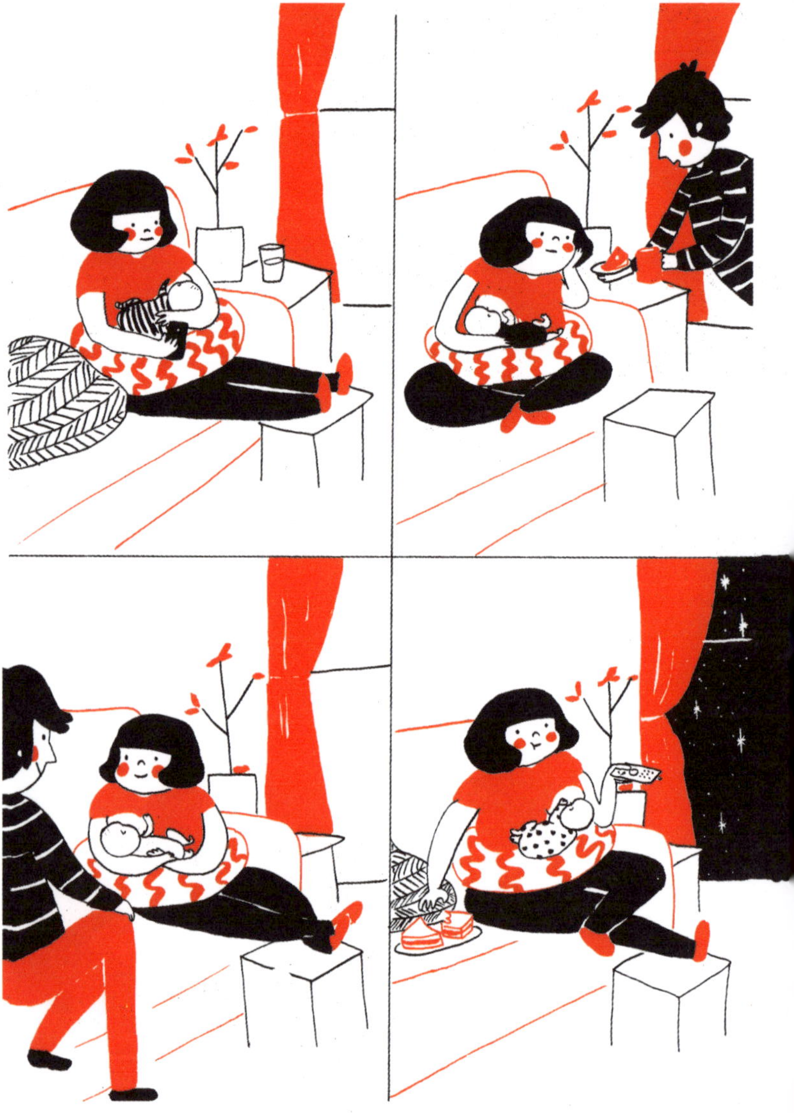

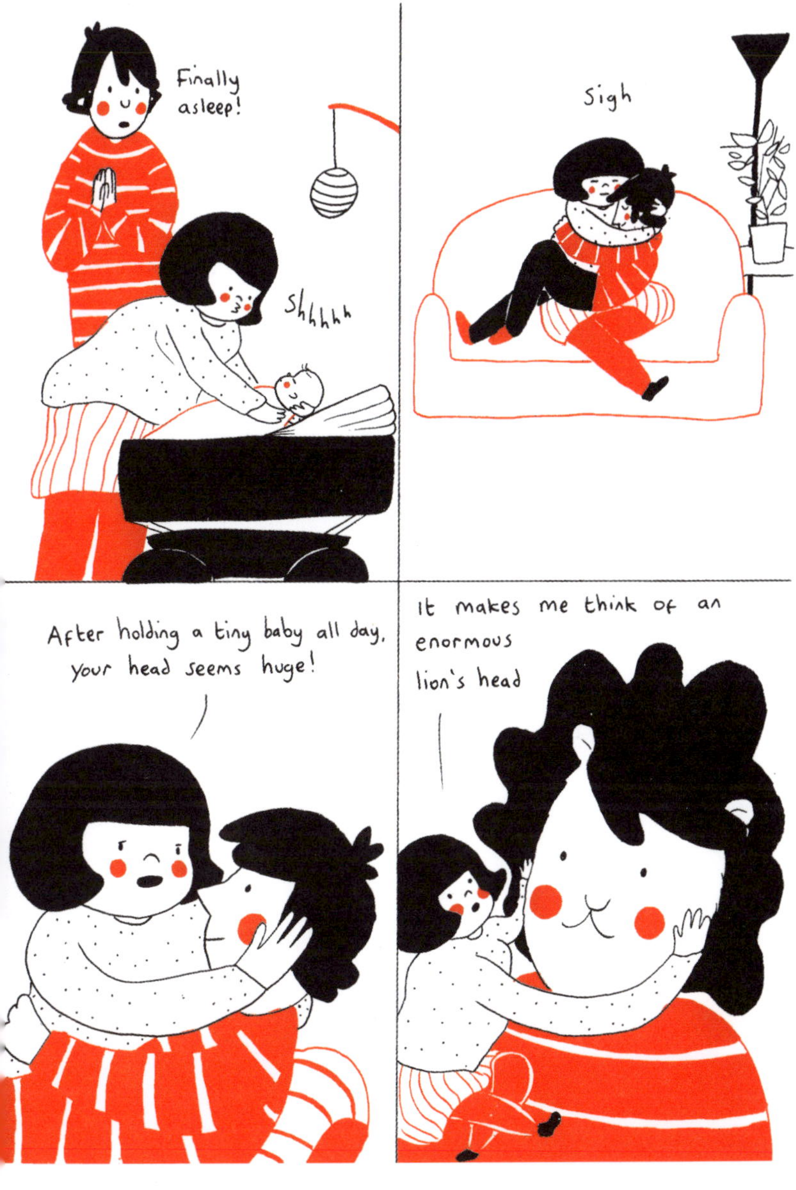
Finally asleep!
Shhhhh
Sigh
After holding a tiny baby all day, your head seems huge!
It makes me think of an enormous lion's head

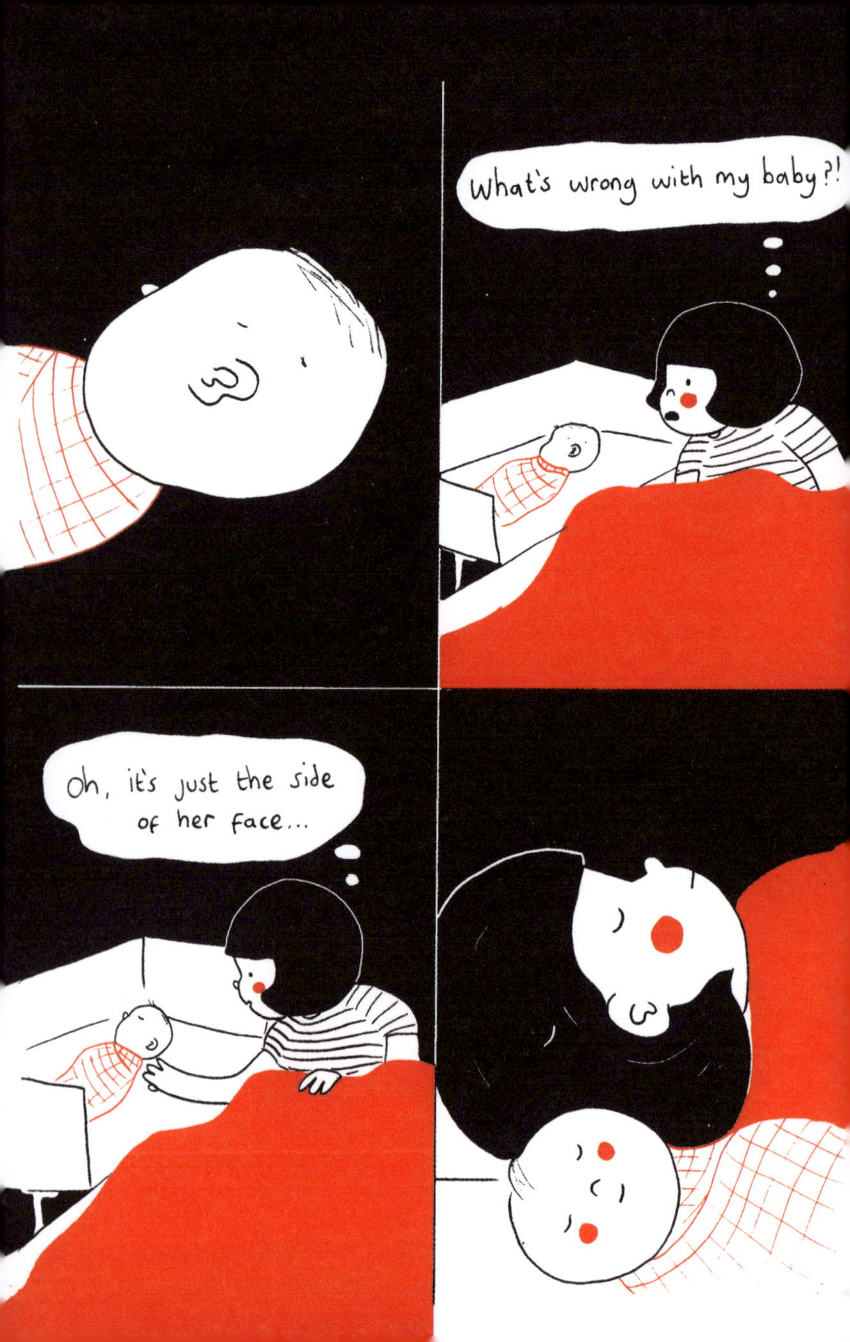
What's wrong with my baby?!
Oh, it's just the side of her face...

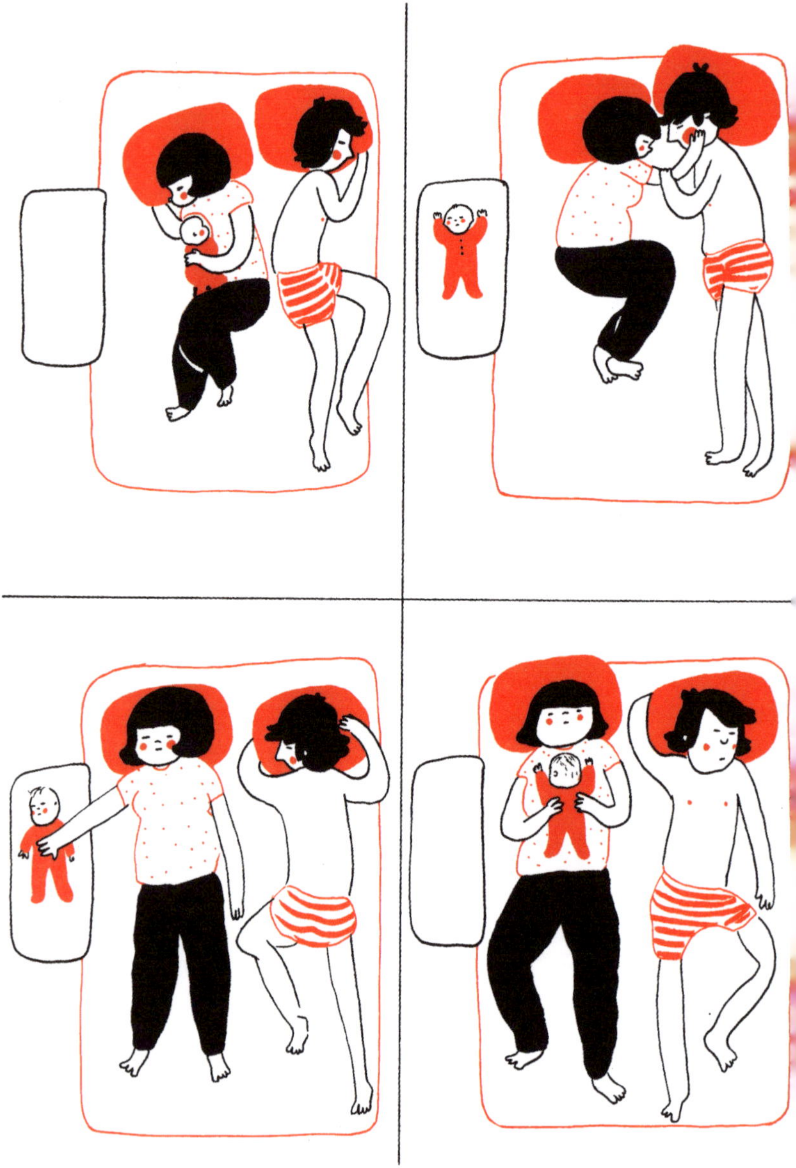

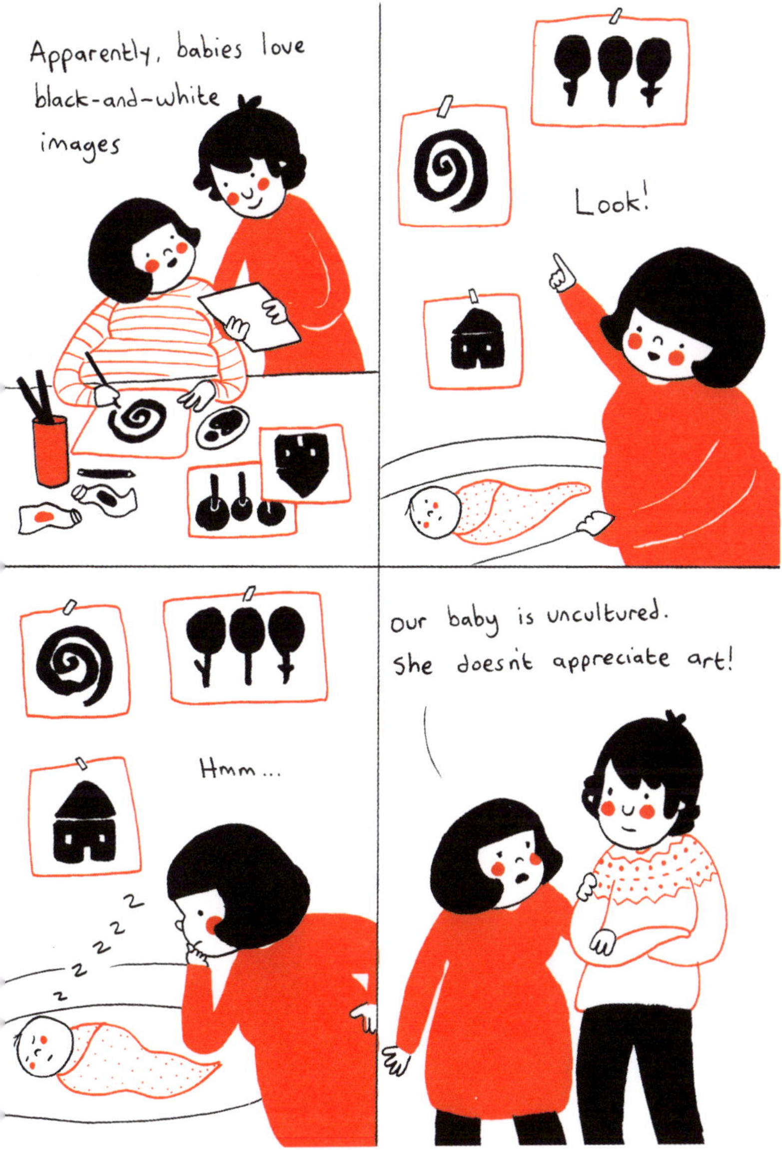
Apparently, babies love black-and-white images
Look!
Hmm...
z z z z z
Our baby is uncultured. She doesn't appreciate art!

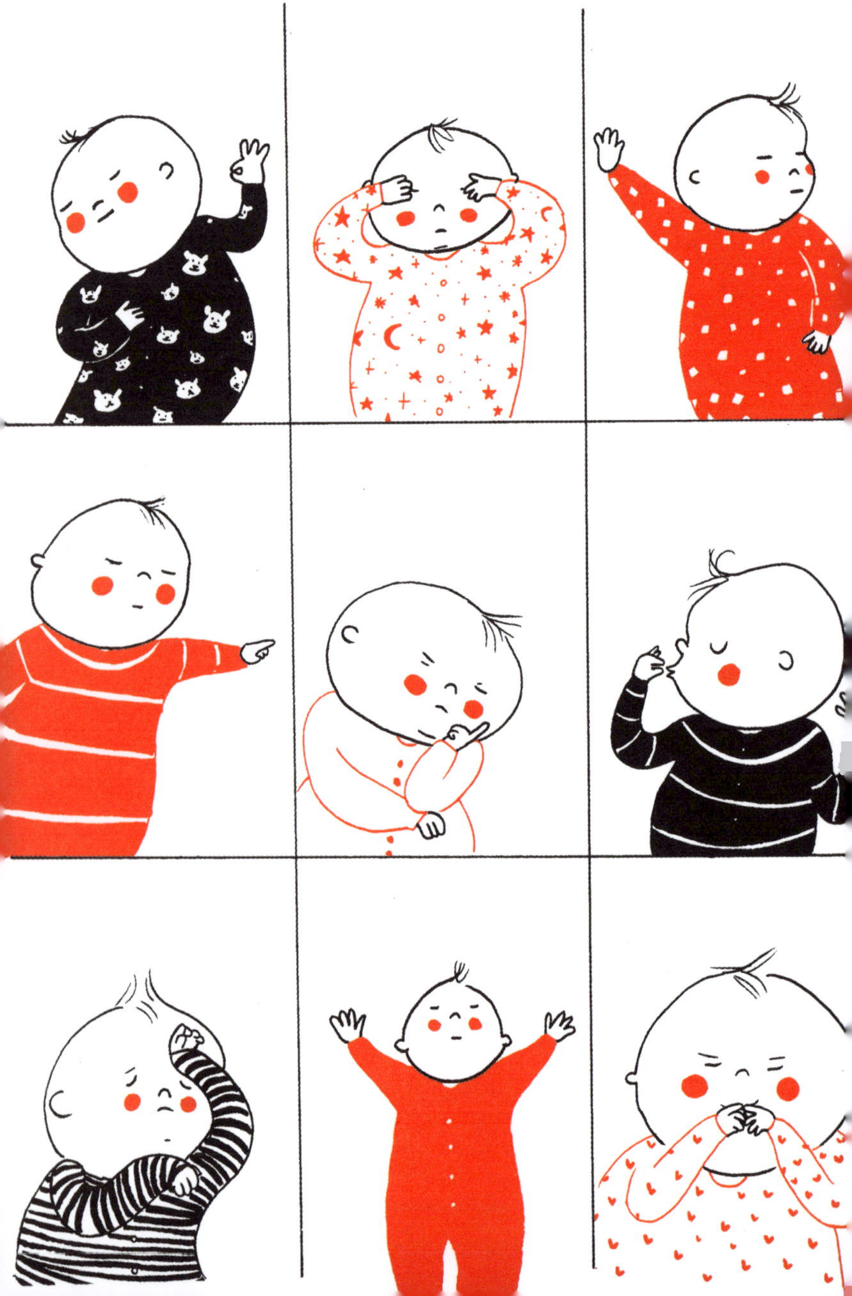

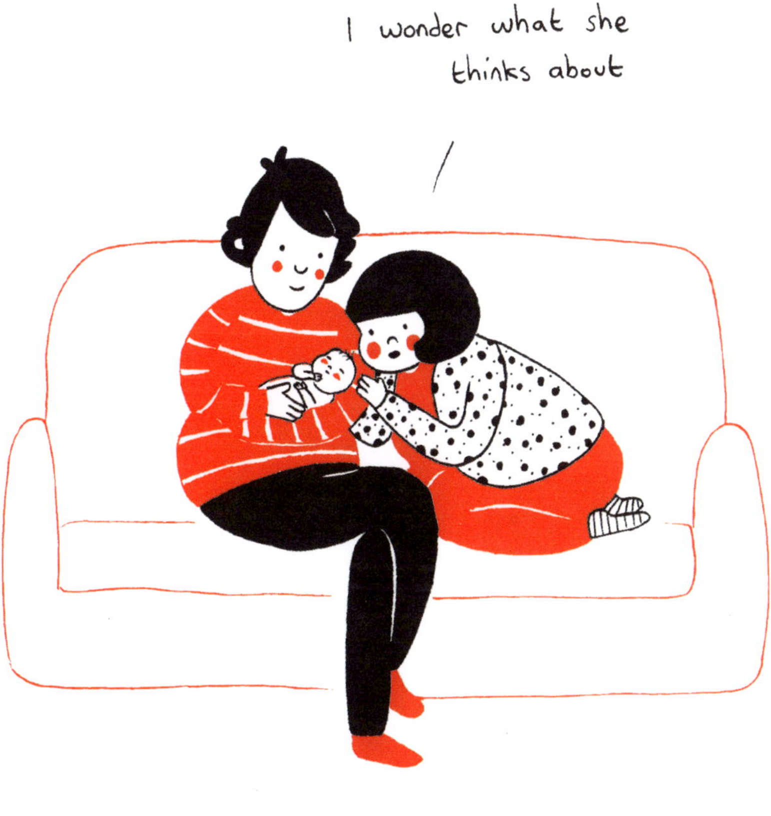
I wonder what she thinks about

Okay, got my TV remotes, got my phone, snacks, book. Everything I need.

I'll just tidy up all this clutter

Shhh Shhh, I know. I'll sit down and feed you right away.

Where's my stuff?!

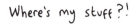

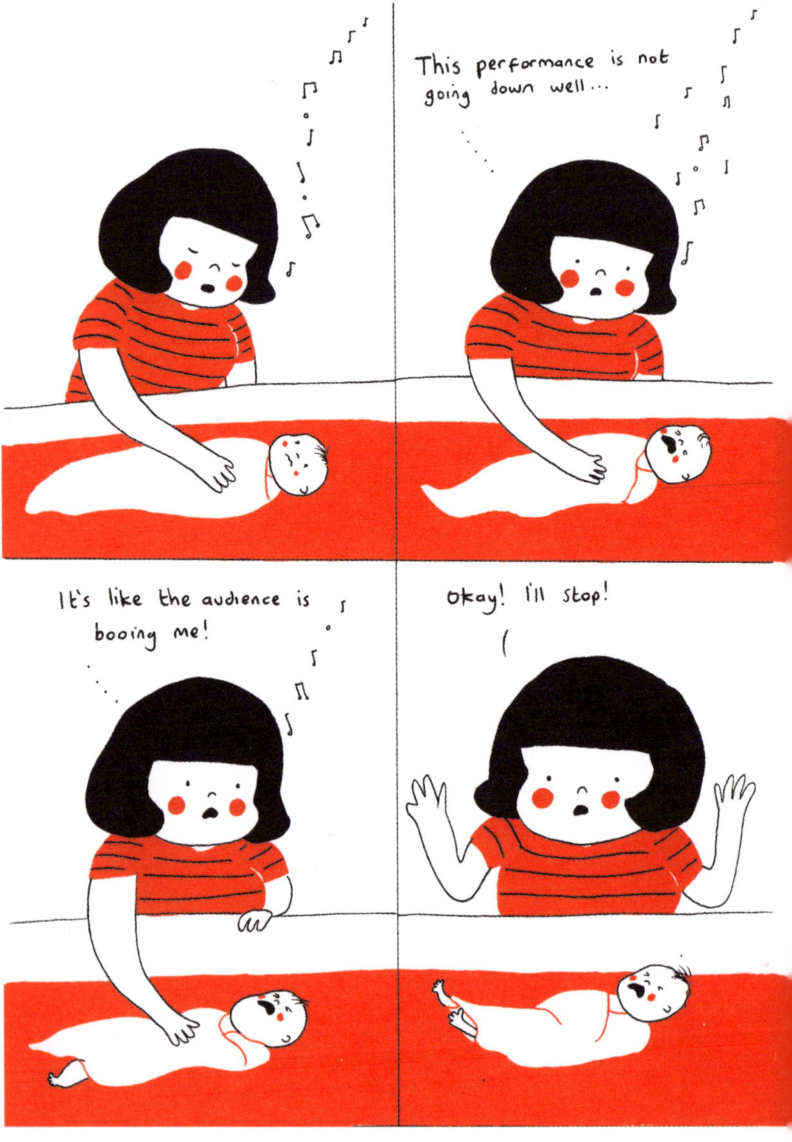
This performance is not going down well...
It's like the audience is booing me!
Okay! I'll stop!

Why am I swaying even though I'm not holding a baby right now?

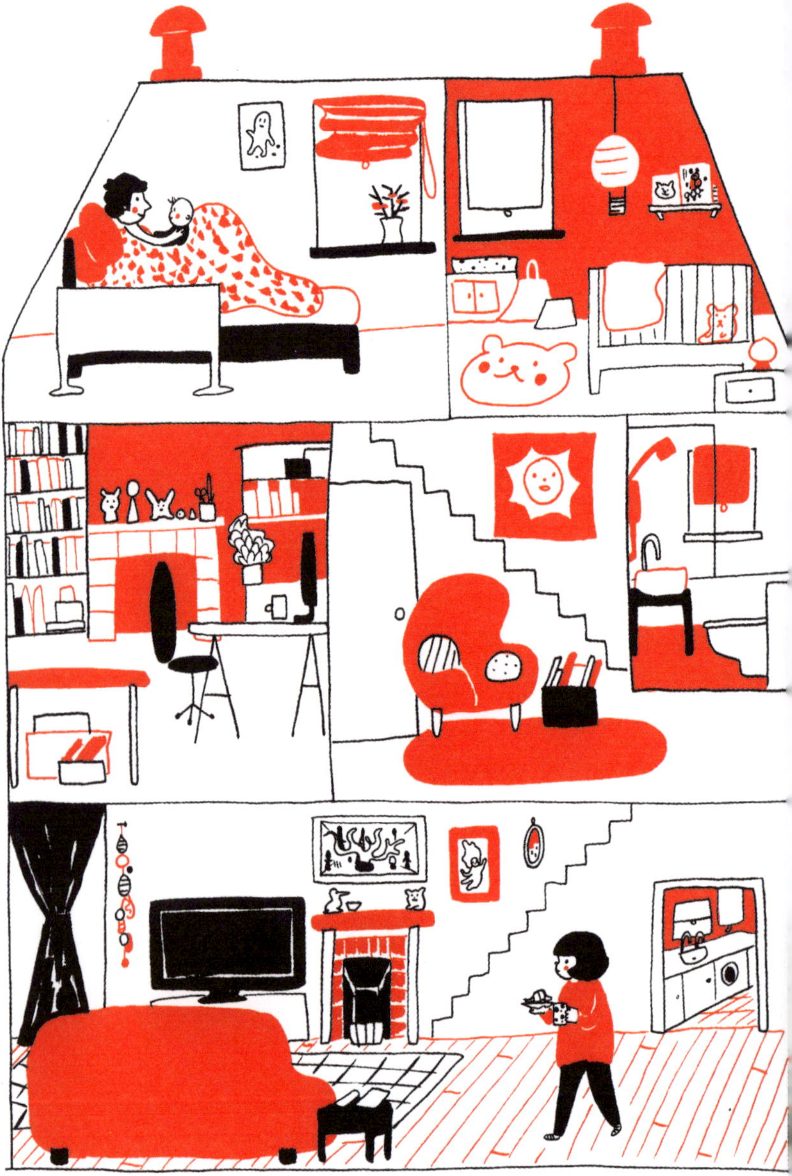

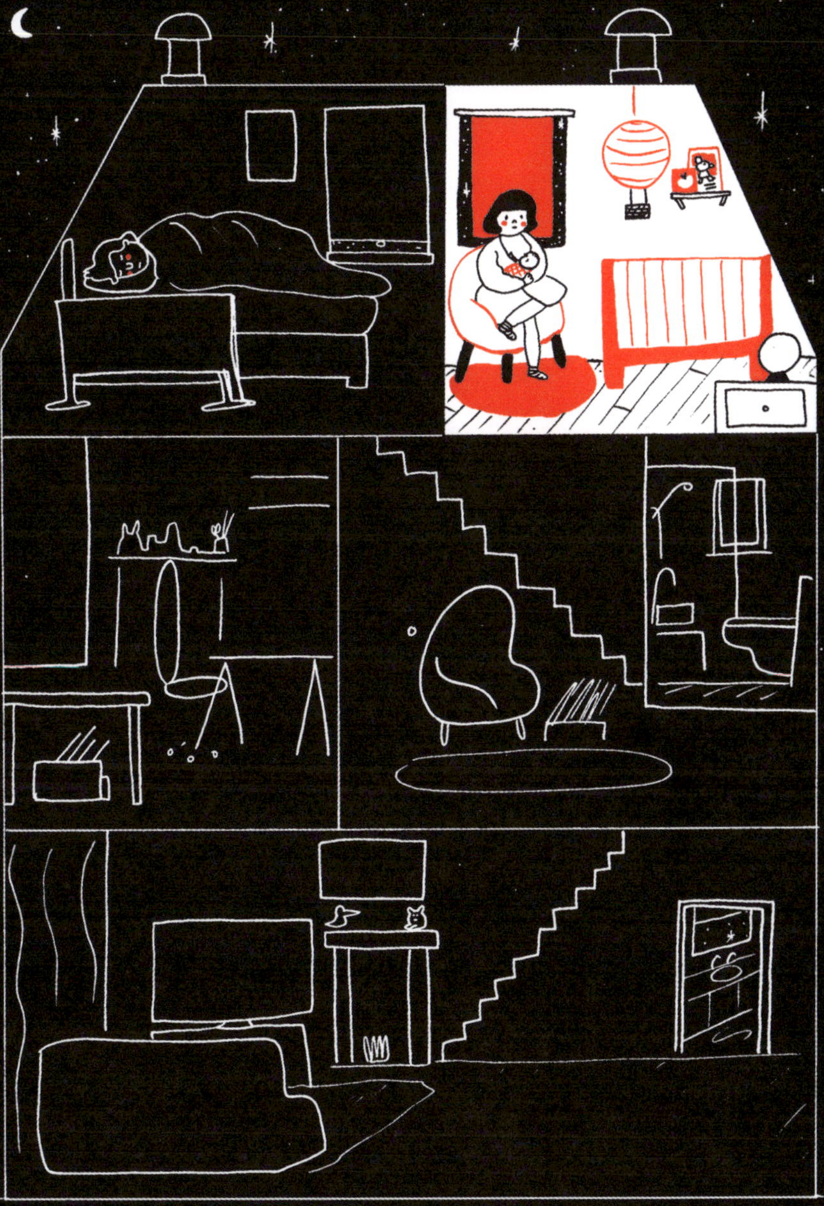

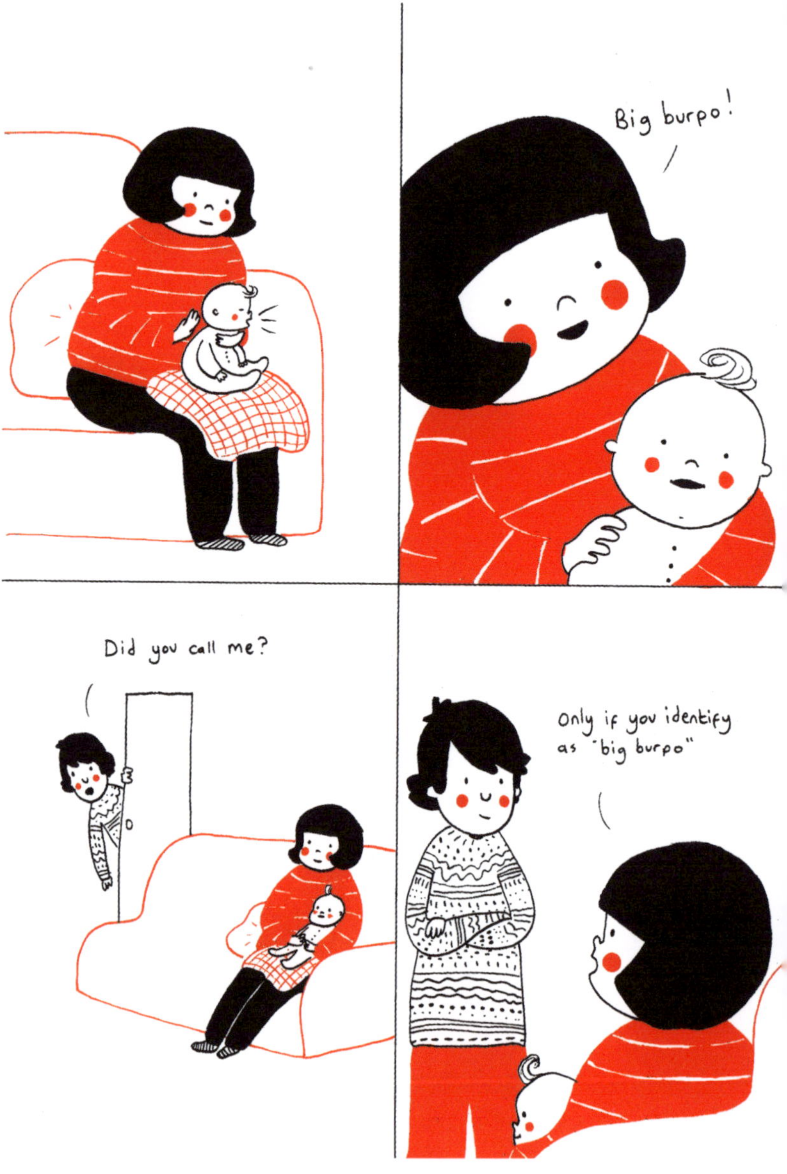
Big burpo!
Did you call me?
Only if you identify as "big burpo"

wWaaaaaaah
AAaaaa
zzzzzzz

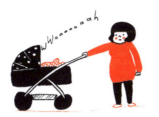

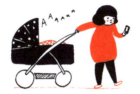

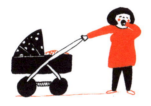

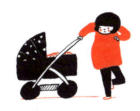

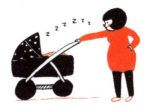

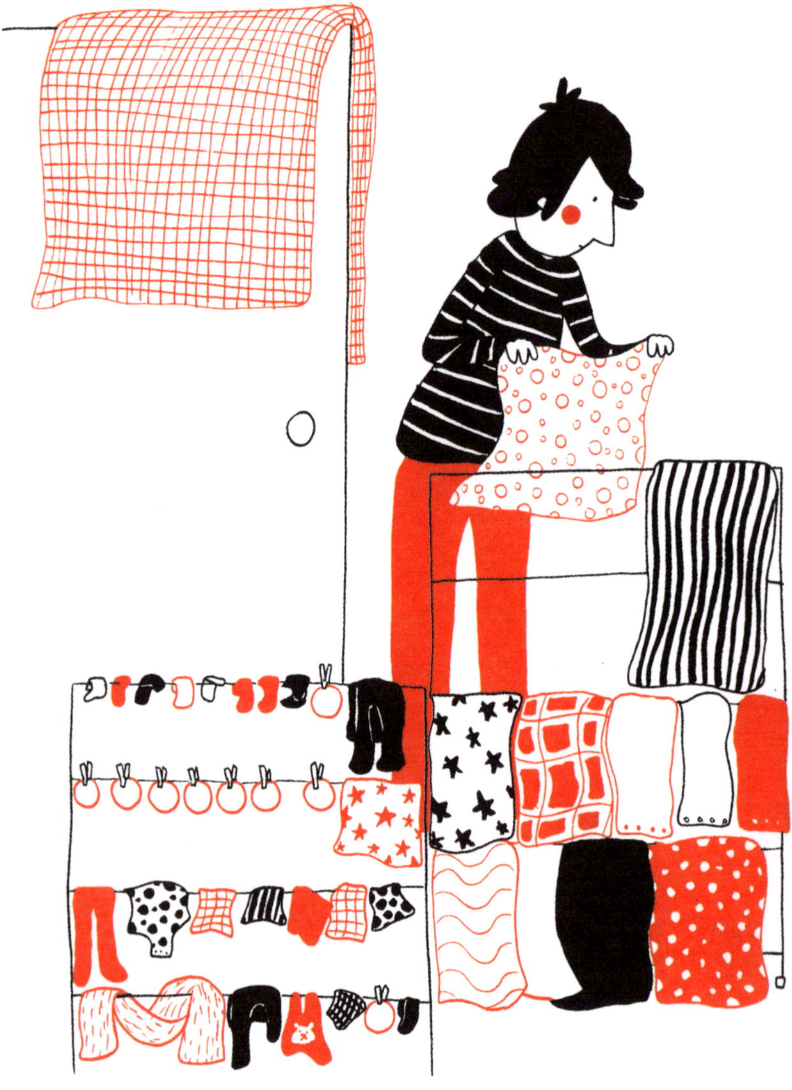

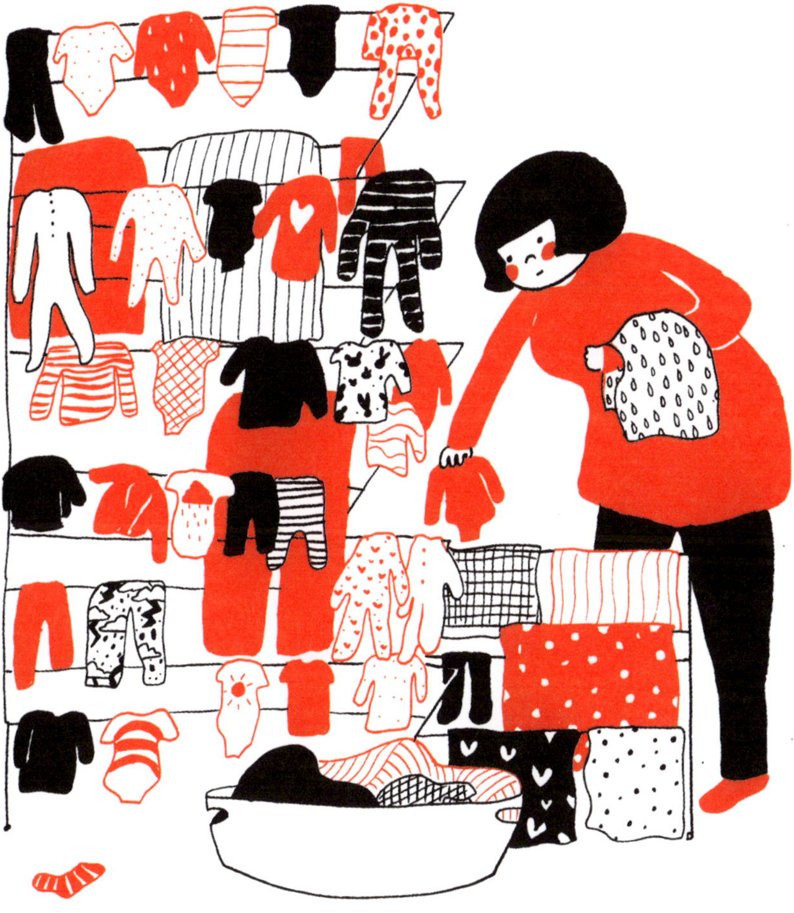

Breastfeeding in public...

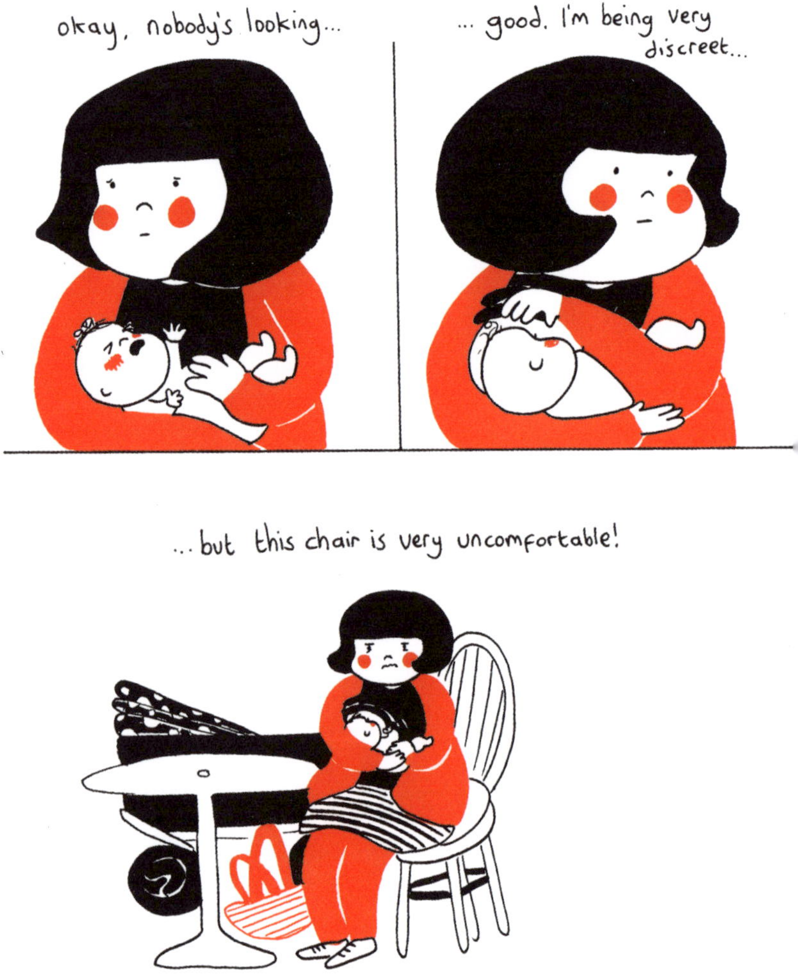
okay, nobody's looking...
... good. I'm being very discreet...
... but this chair is very uncomfortable!

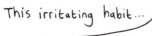

This irritating habit...

Will this be warm enough for her today?

What time should she nap?

Where shall I put this?

Do you know how—

STOP asking me ABOUT EVERY TINY THING!

Figure it out yourself!

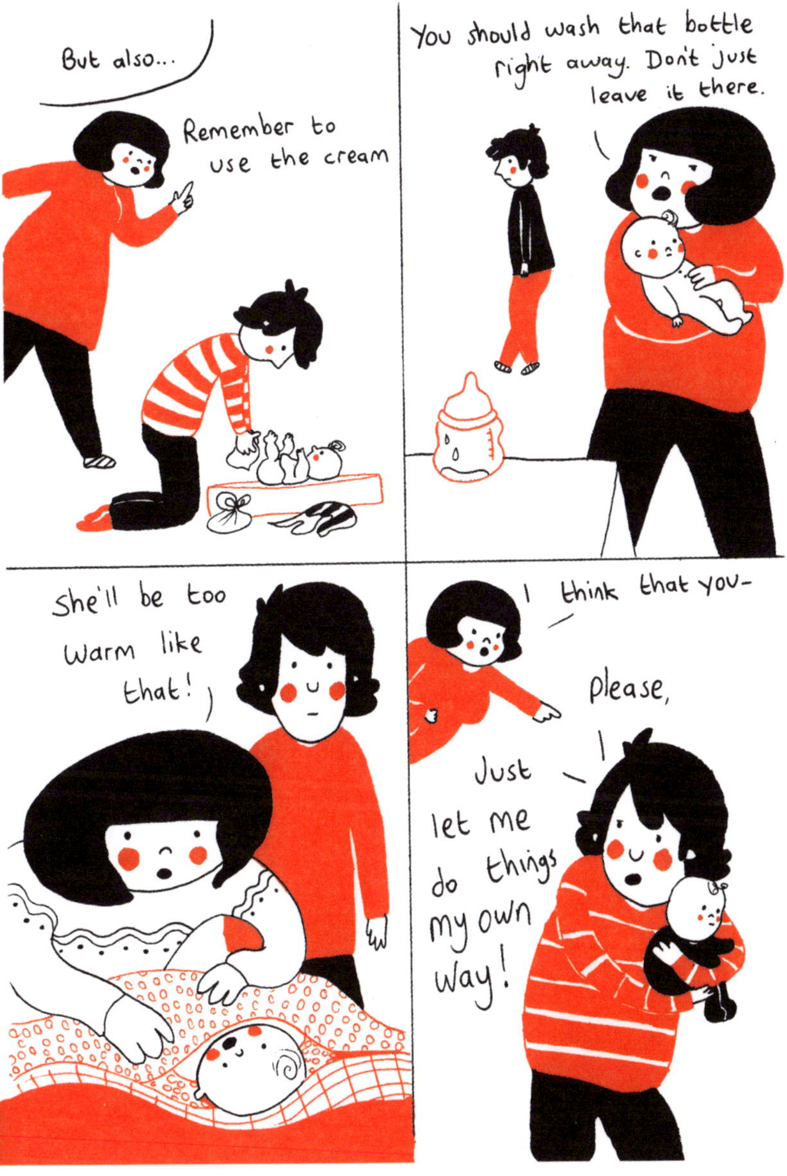
But also...
Remember to use the cream
You should wash that bottle right away. Don't just leave it there.
She'll be too warm like that!
I think that you-
Please,
Just let me do things my own way!

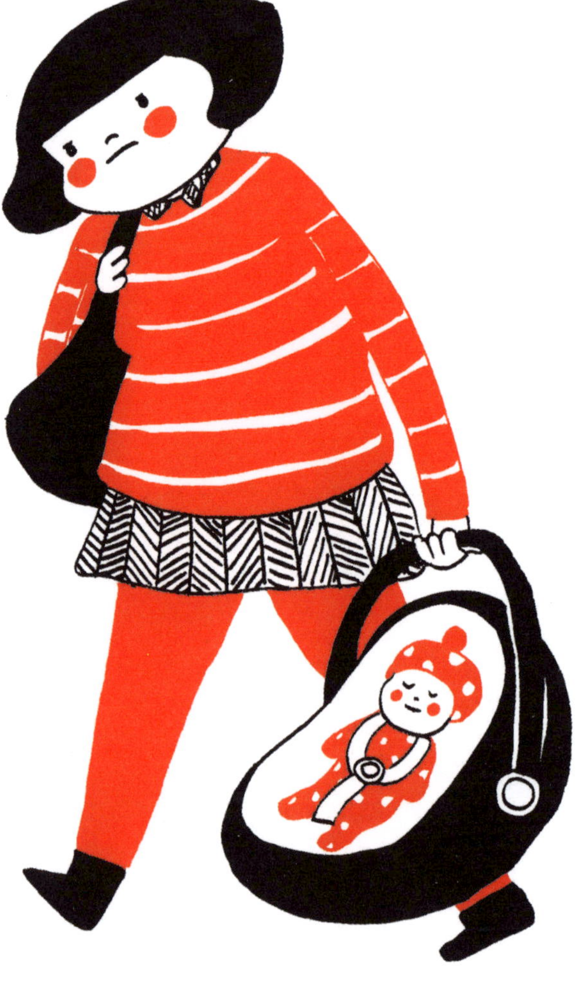

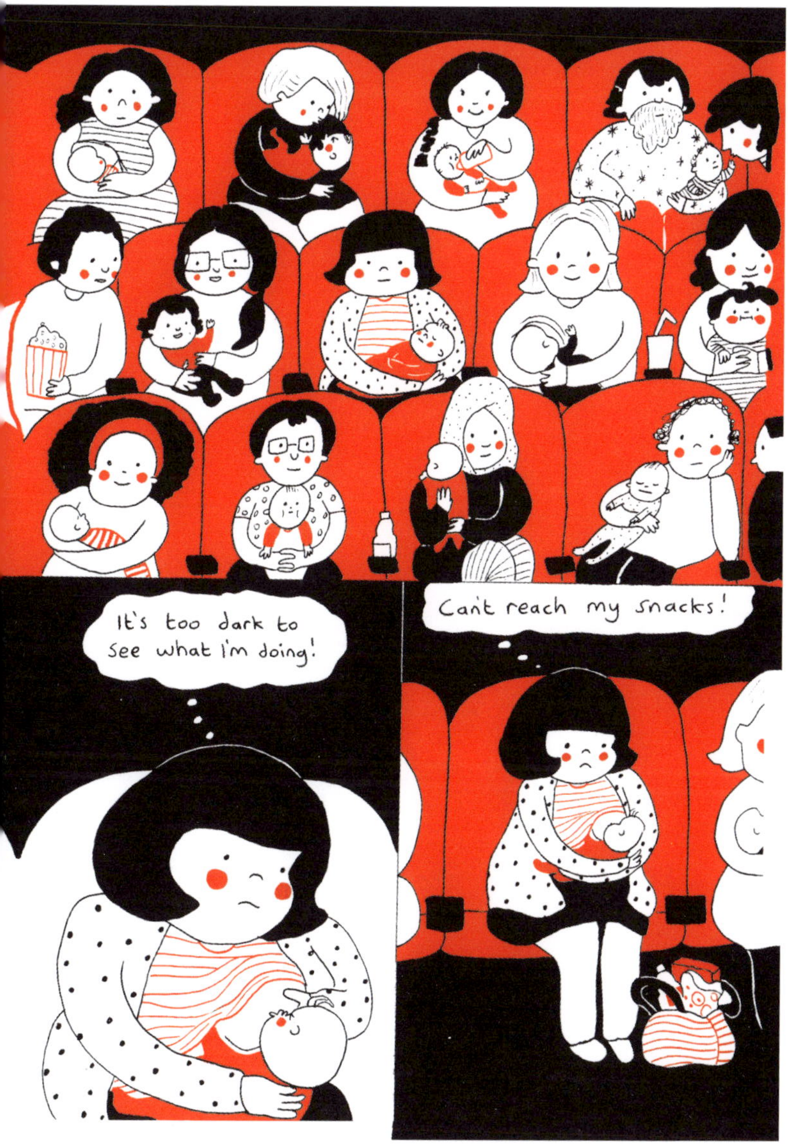
It's too dark to see what I'm doing!
Can't reach my snacks!

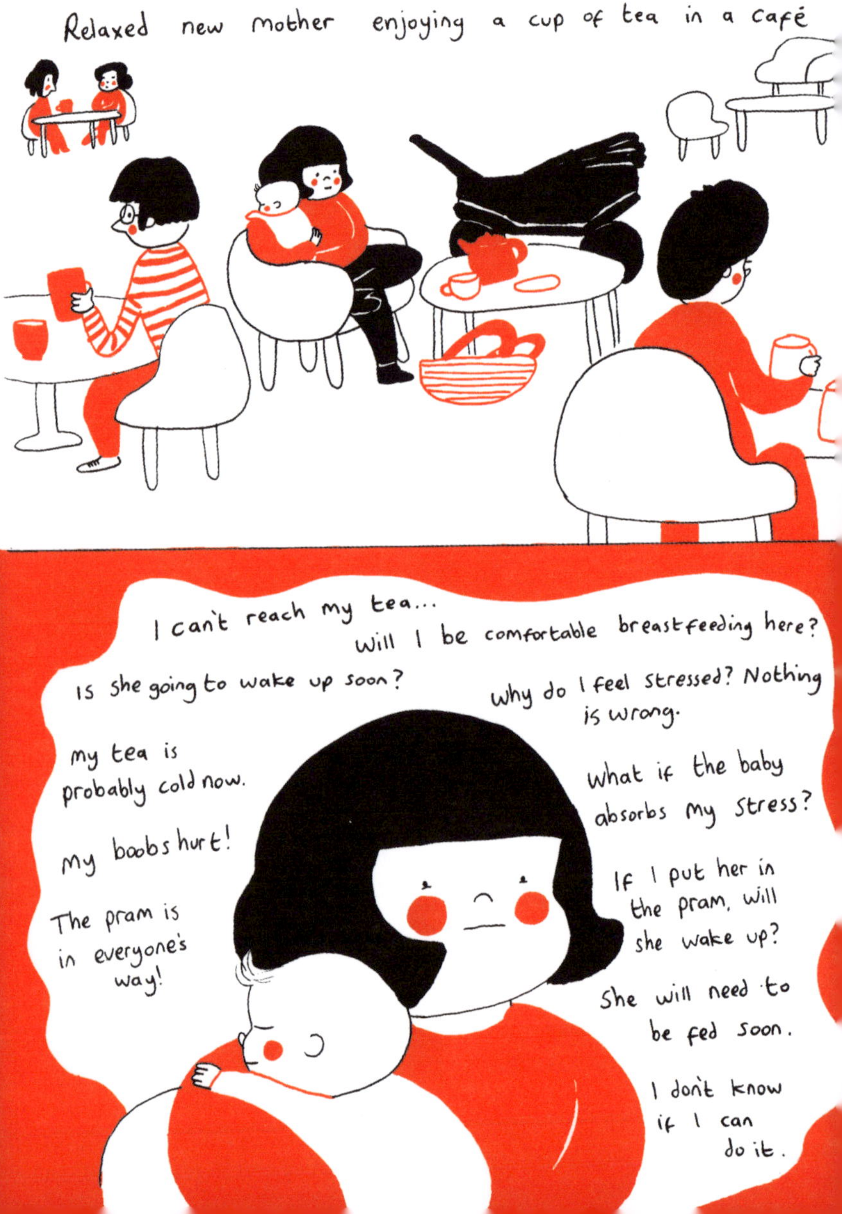
Relaxed new mother enjoying a cup of tea in a café
I can't reach my tea...
Will I be comfortable breastfeeding here?
Is she going to wake up soon?
Why do I feel stressed? Nothing is wrong.
My tea is probably cold now.
What if the baby absorbs my stress?
My boobs hurt!
If I put her in the pram, will she wake up?
The pram is in everyone's way!
She will need to be fed soon.
I don't know if I can do it.

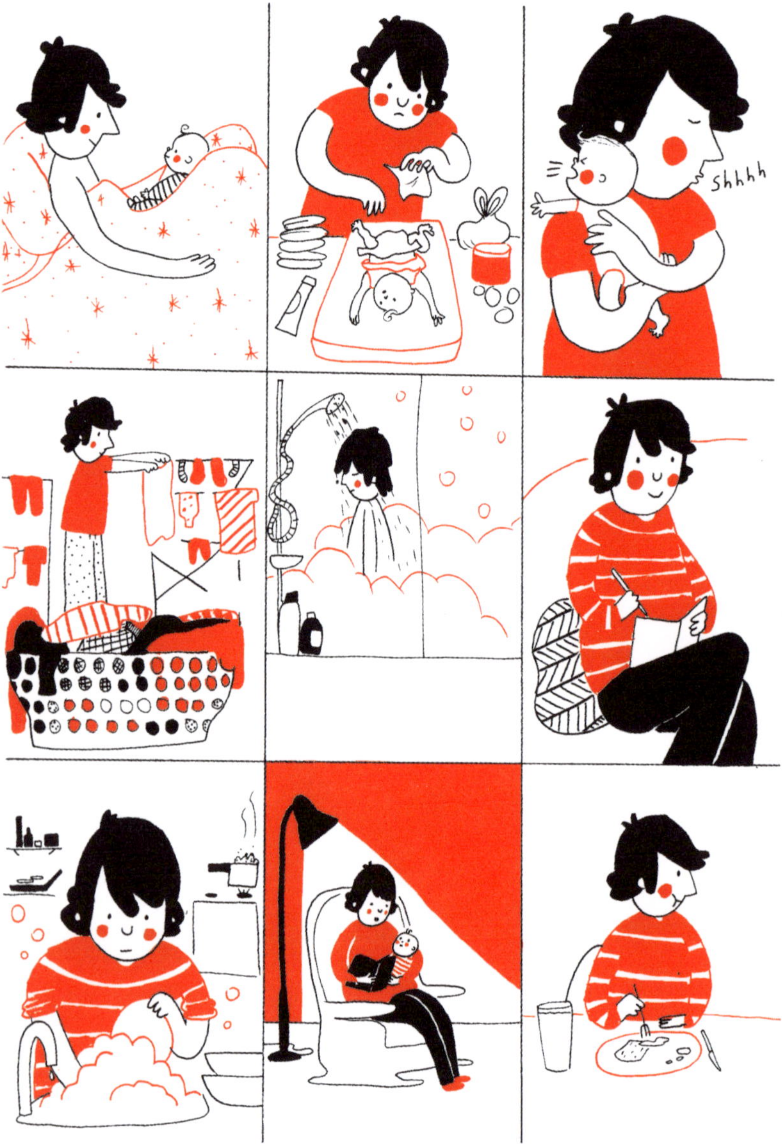
Shhhh

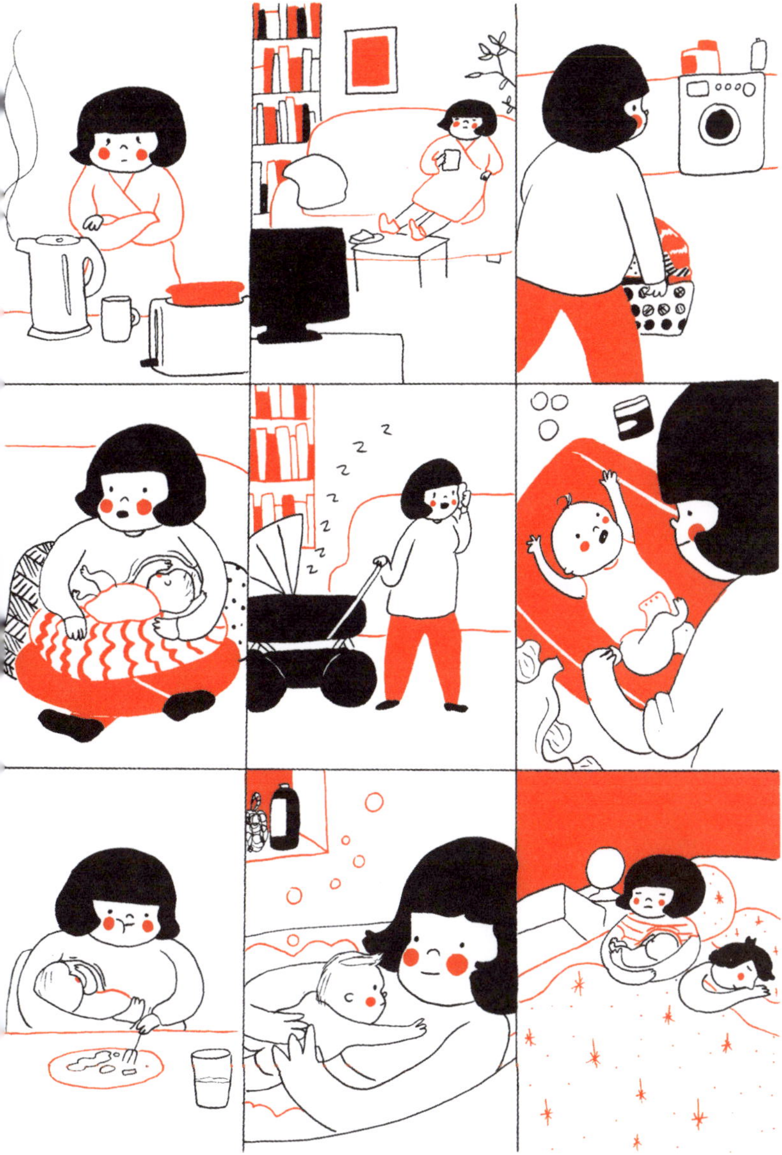
z z z z z z z

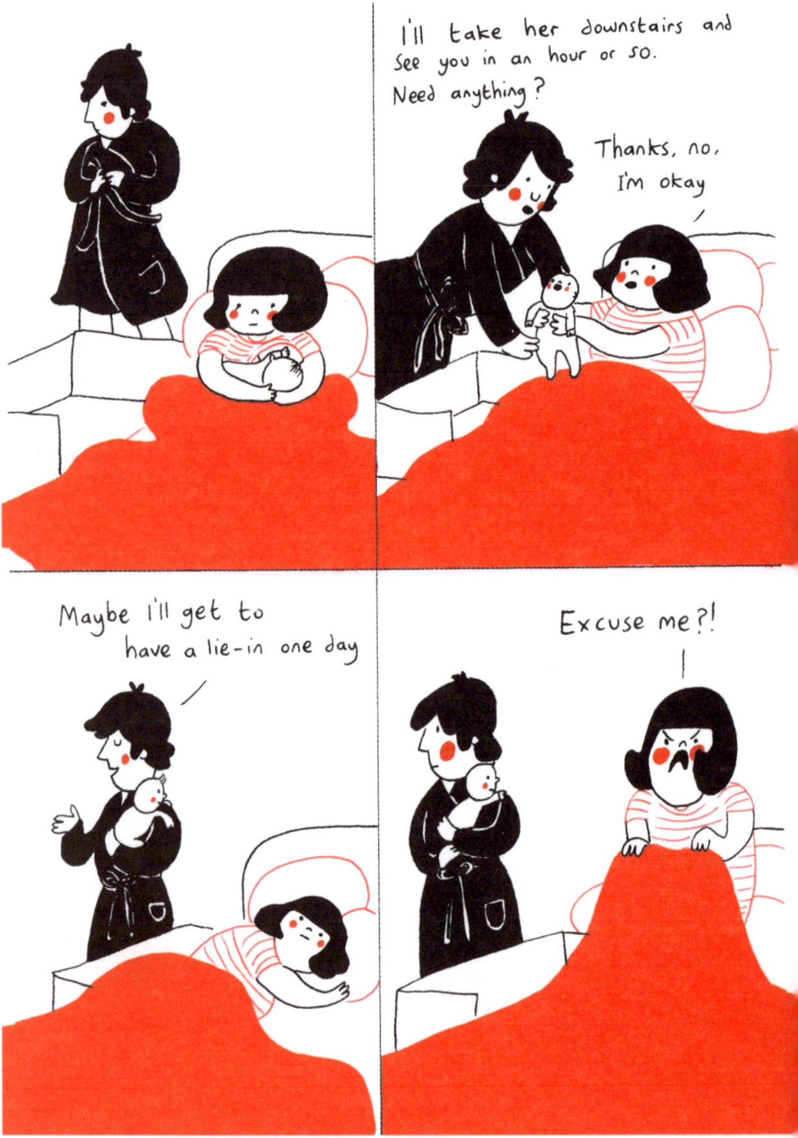
I'll take her downstairs and see you in an hour or so. Need anything?
Thanks, no, I'm okay
Maybe I'll get to have a lie-in one day
Excuse me?!

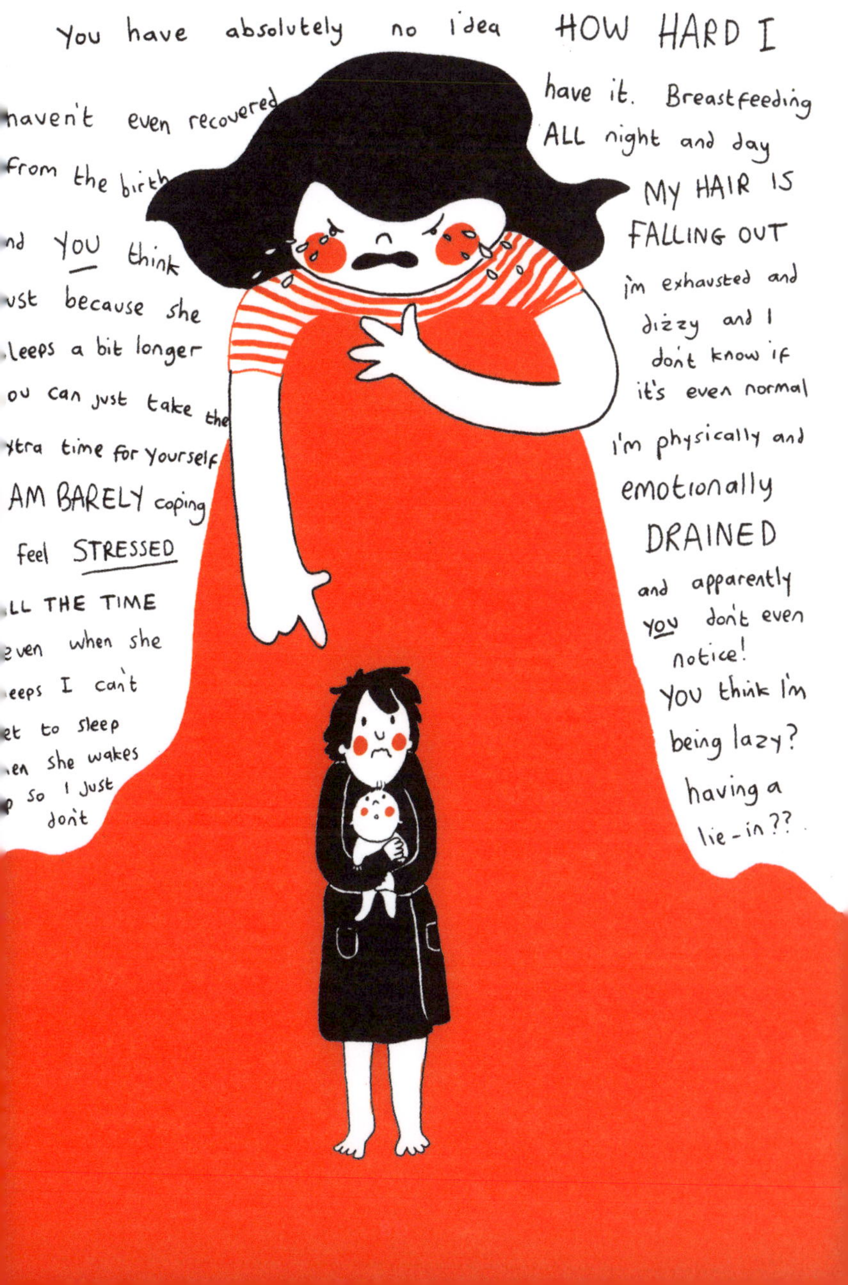
You have absolutely no idea HOW HARD I have it. Breastfeeding ALL night and day
MY HAIR IS FALLING OUT
i'm exhausted and dizzy and I don't know if it's even normal
i'm physically and emotionally DRAINED
and apparently YOU don't even notice!
You think i'm being lazy?
having a lie-in??
haven't even recovered from the birth
nd YOU think
ust because she
leeps a bit longer
ou can just take the
xtra time for yourself
AM BARELY coping
feel STRESSED
LL THE TIME
even when she
eeps I can't
et to sleep
en she wakes
p so I just
don't

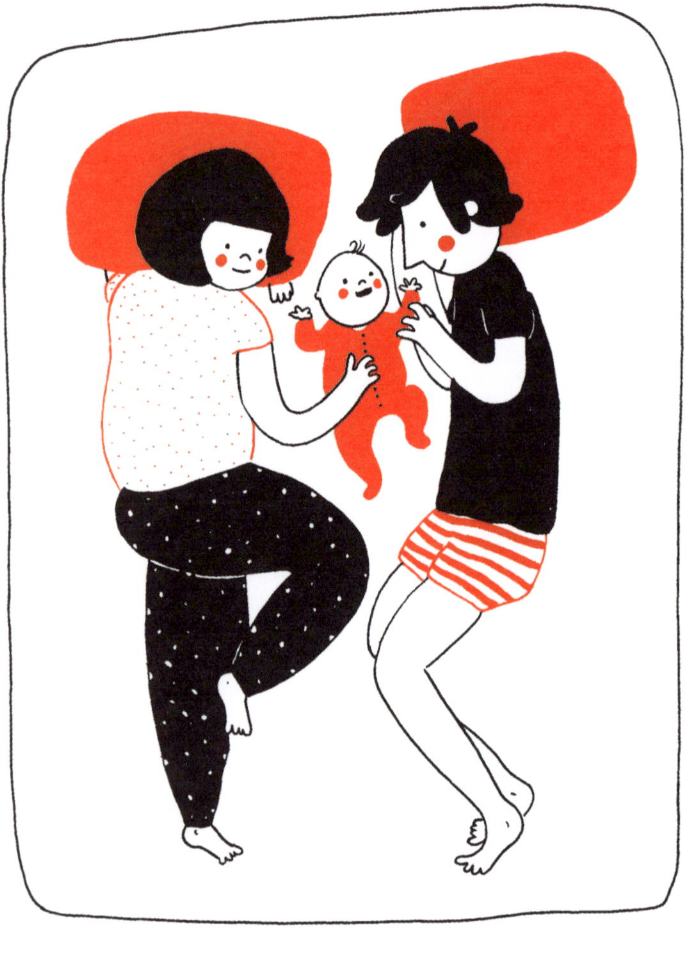

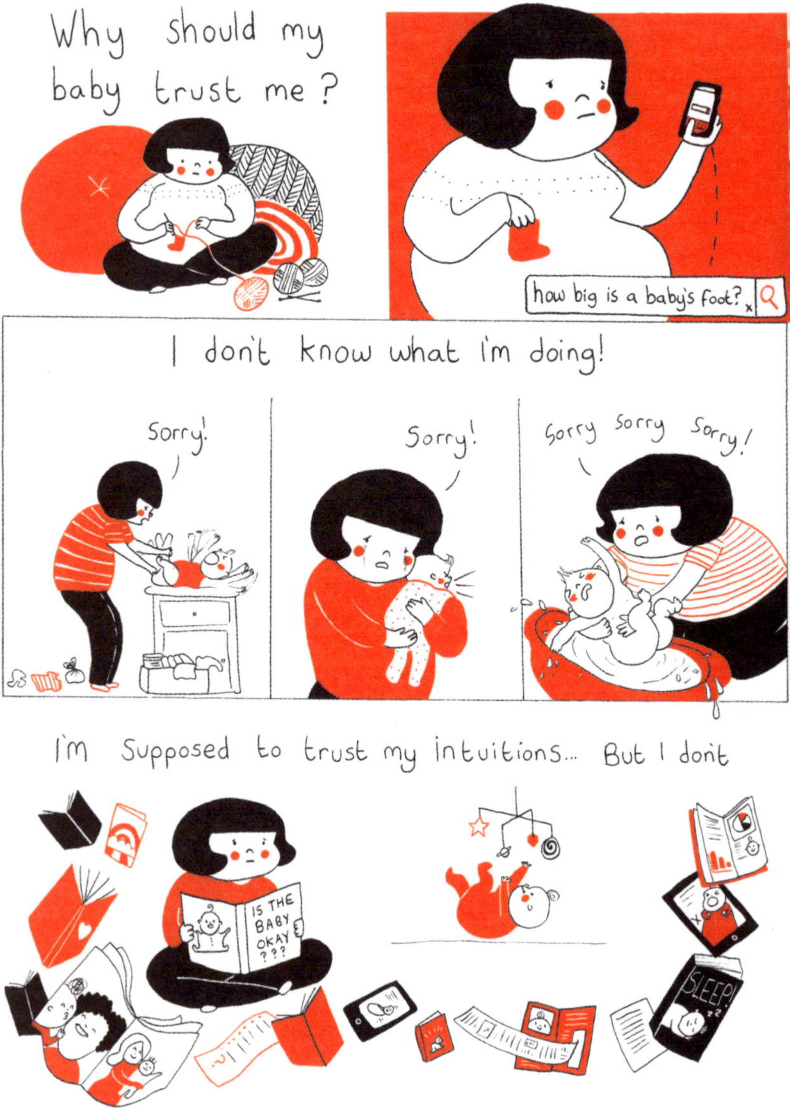
Why should my baby trust me?
how big is a baby's foot?
I don't know what I'm doing!
Sorry!
Sorry!
Sorry Sorry Sorry!
I'm supposed to trust my intuitions... But I don't
IS THE BABY OKAY ???
SLEEP!

Why would anyone trust me?

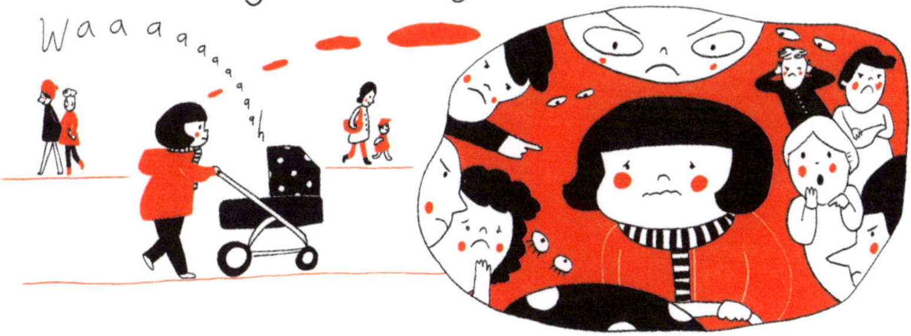
Waaaaaaaaaaaah

My own brain doesn't even trust me!

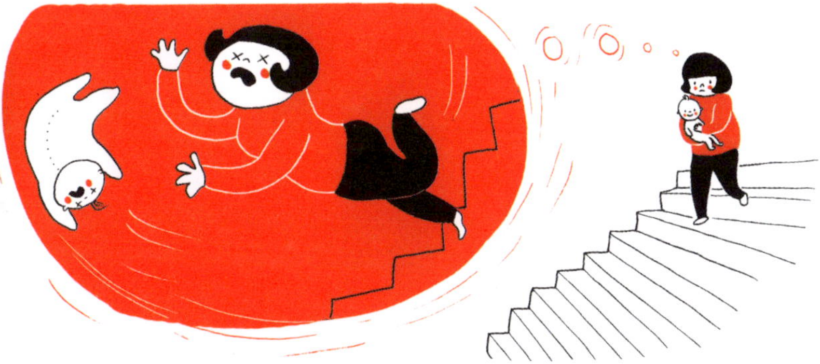

But I can trust others and it really helps.

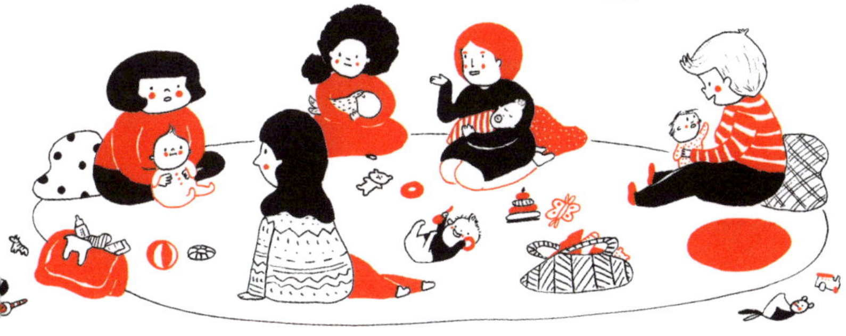

she rolled!

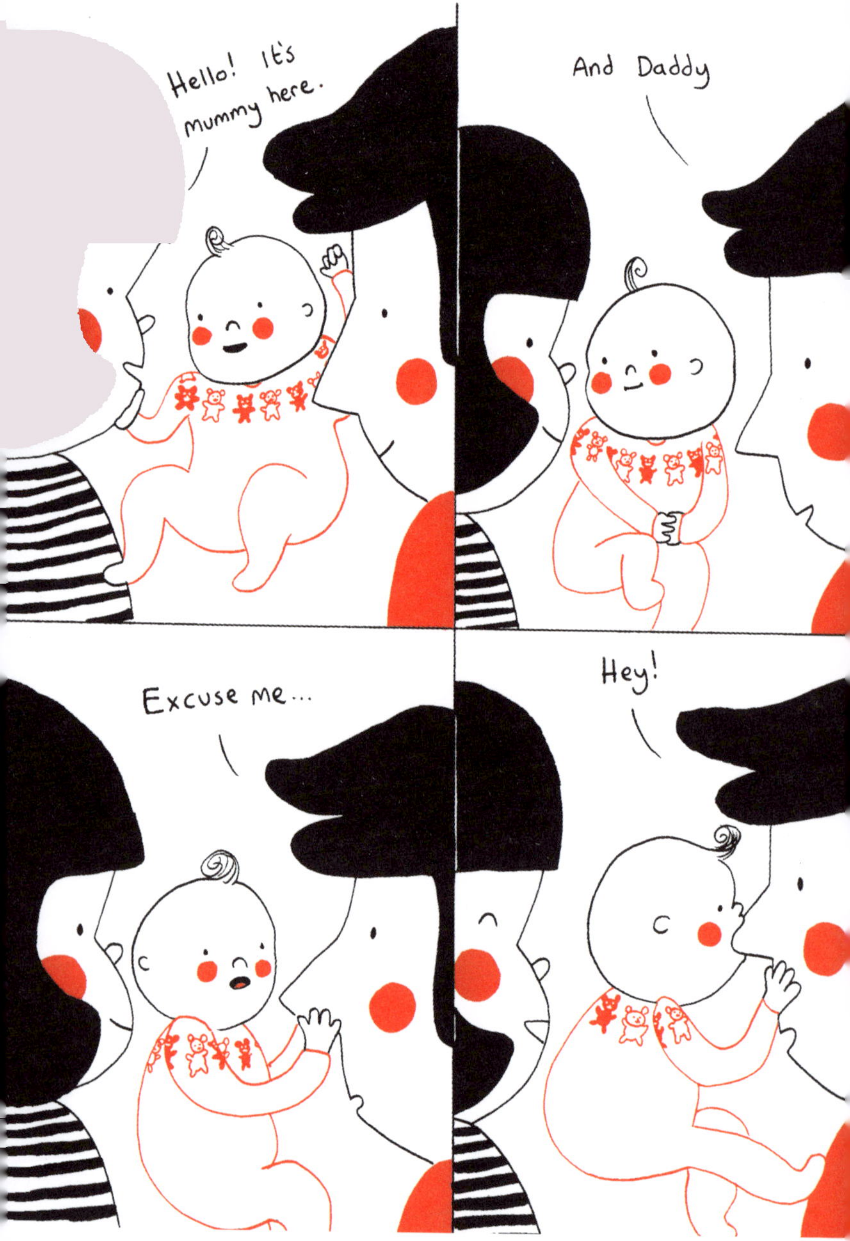
Hello! It's Mummy here.
And Daddy
Excuse me...
Hey!

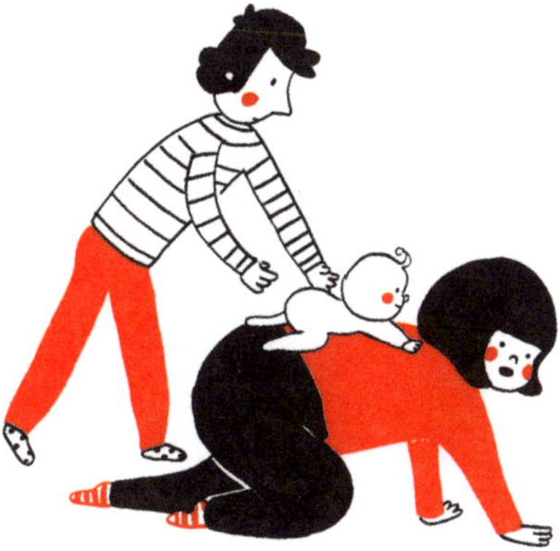

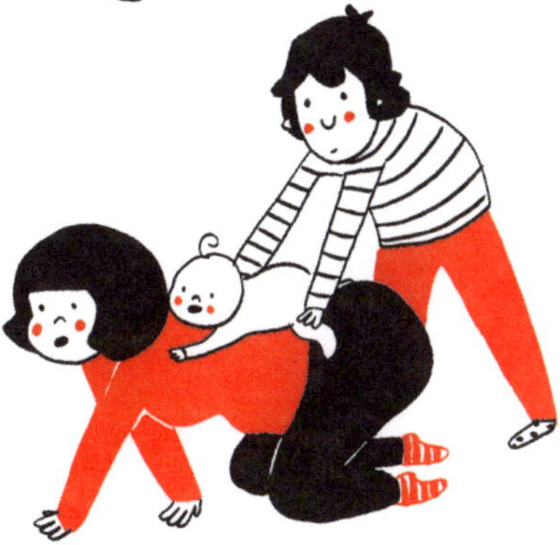

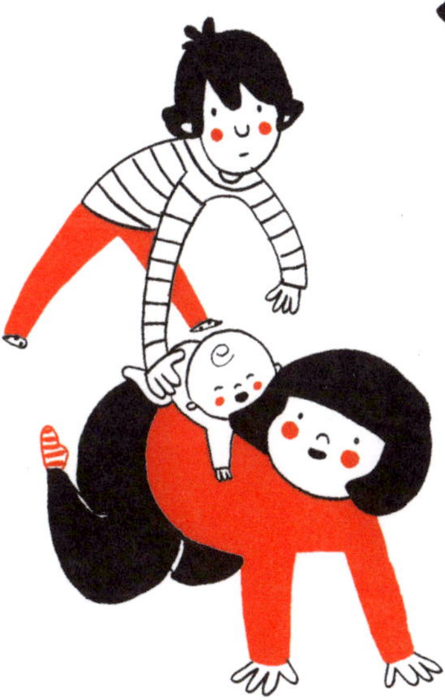

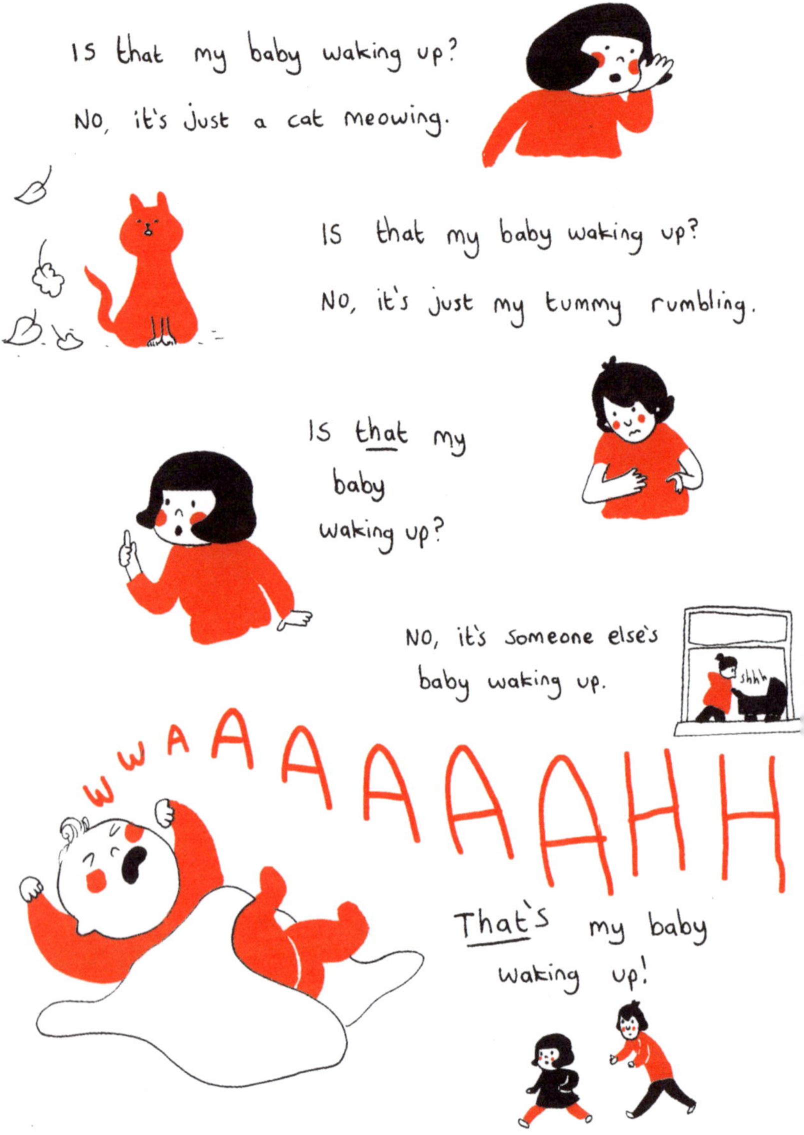
Is that my baby waking up?
No, it's just a cat meowing.
Is that my baby waking up?
No, it's just my tummy rumbling.
Is that my baby waking up?
No, it's someone else's baby waking up.
shhh
WWAAAAAAAAHH
That's my baby waking up!

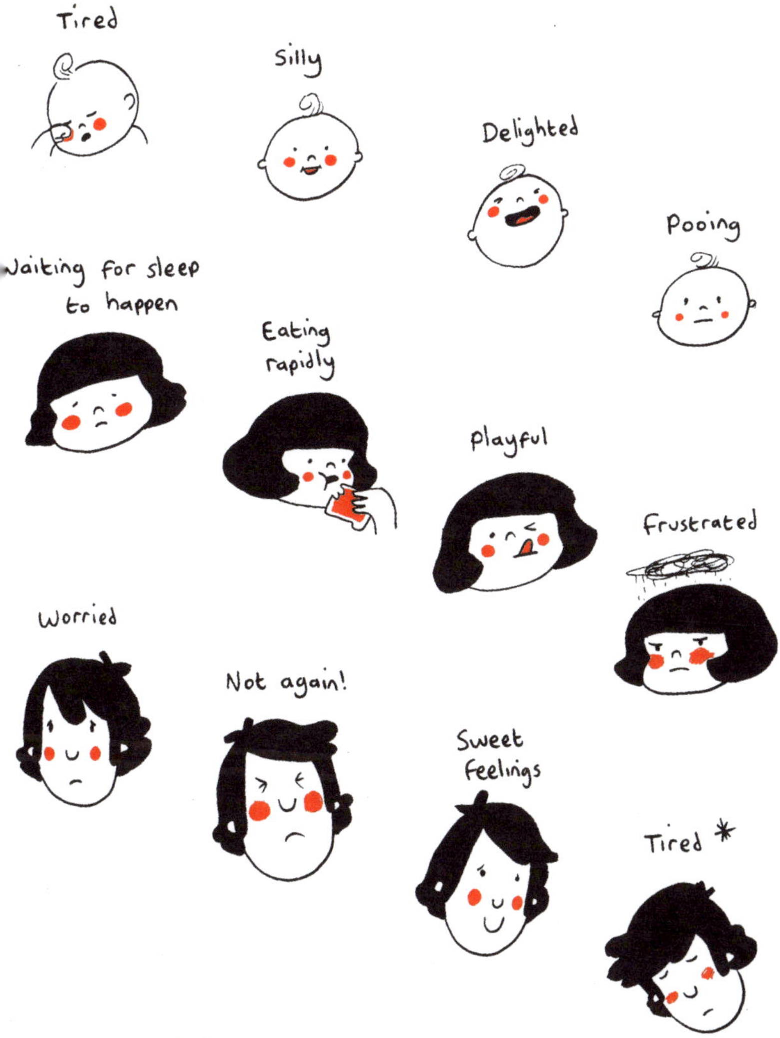
Tired
Silly
Delighted
Pooing
Waiting for sleep to happen
Eating rapidly
Playful
Frustrated
Worried
Not again!
Sweet feelings
Tired *

* Not as tired as you, but still tired

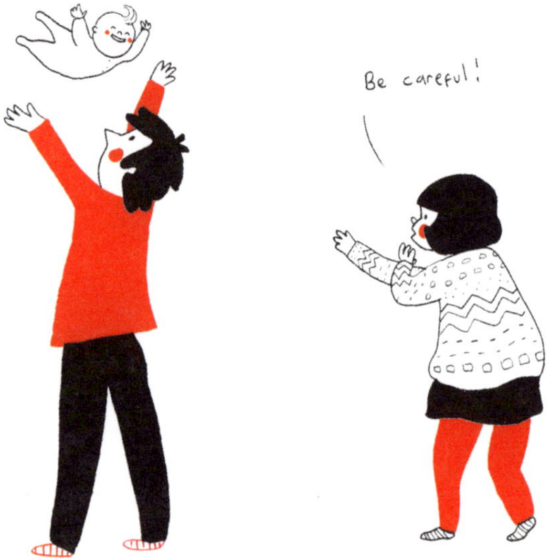
Be careful!

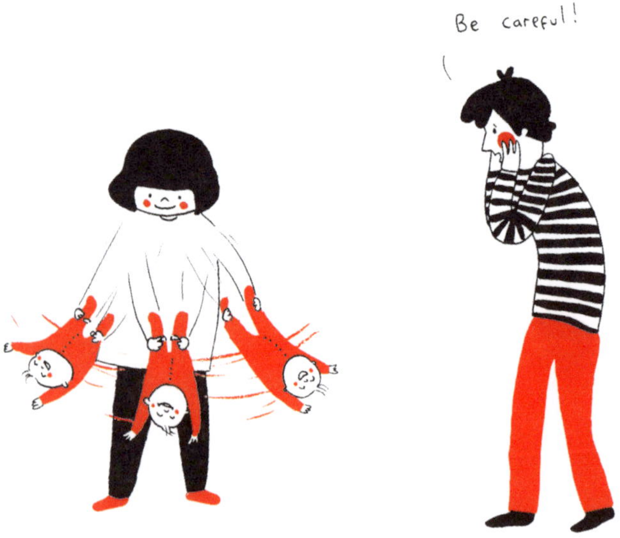
Be careful!

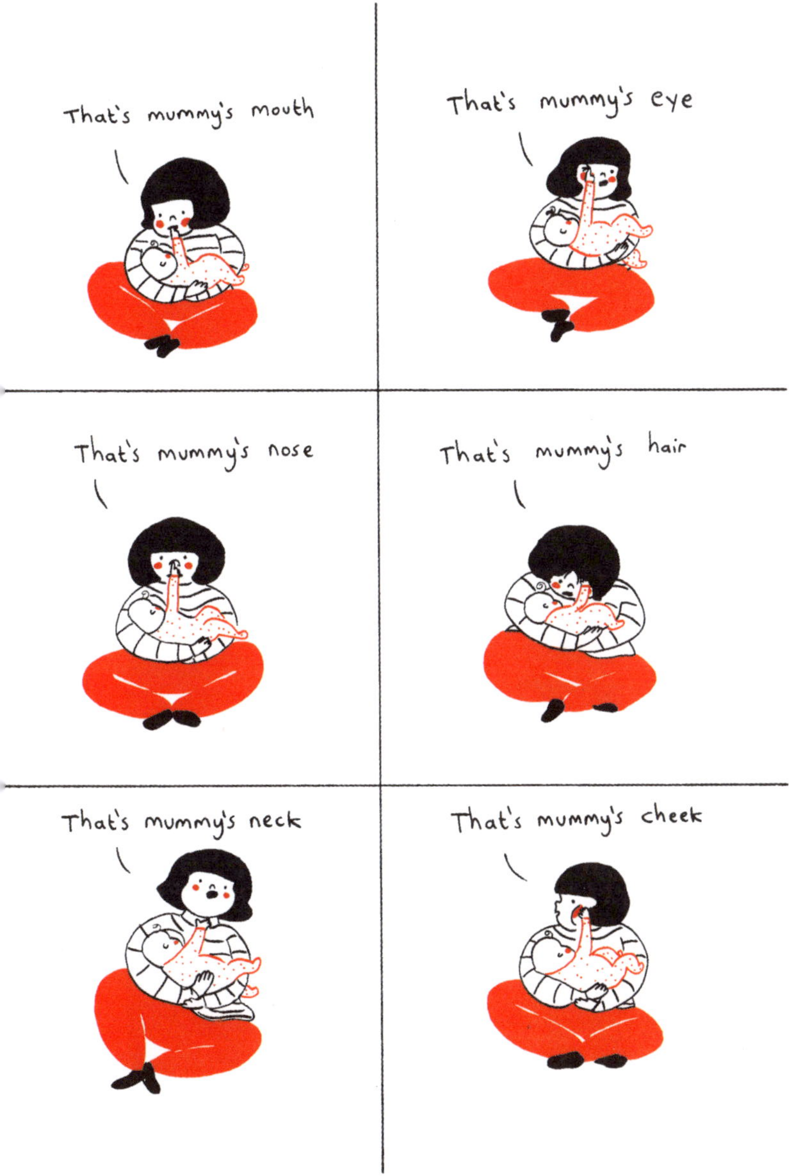
That's mummy's mouth
That's mummy's eye
That's mummy's nose
That's mummy's hair
That's mummy's neck
That's mummy's cheek

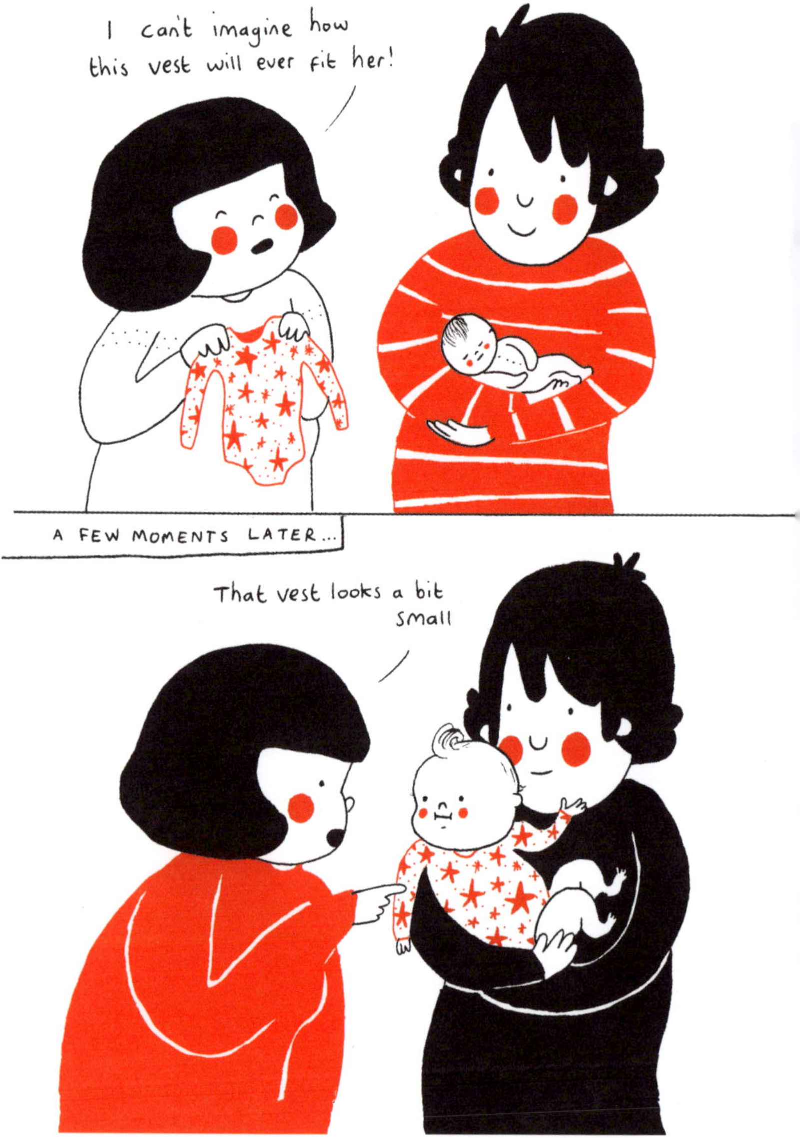
I can't imagine how this vest will ever fit her!
A FEW MOMENTS LATER...
That vest looks a bit small

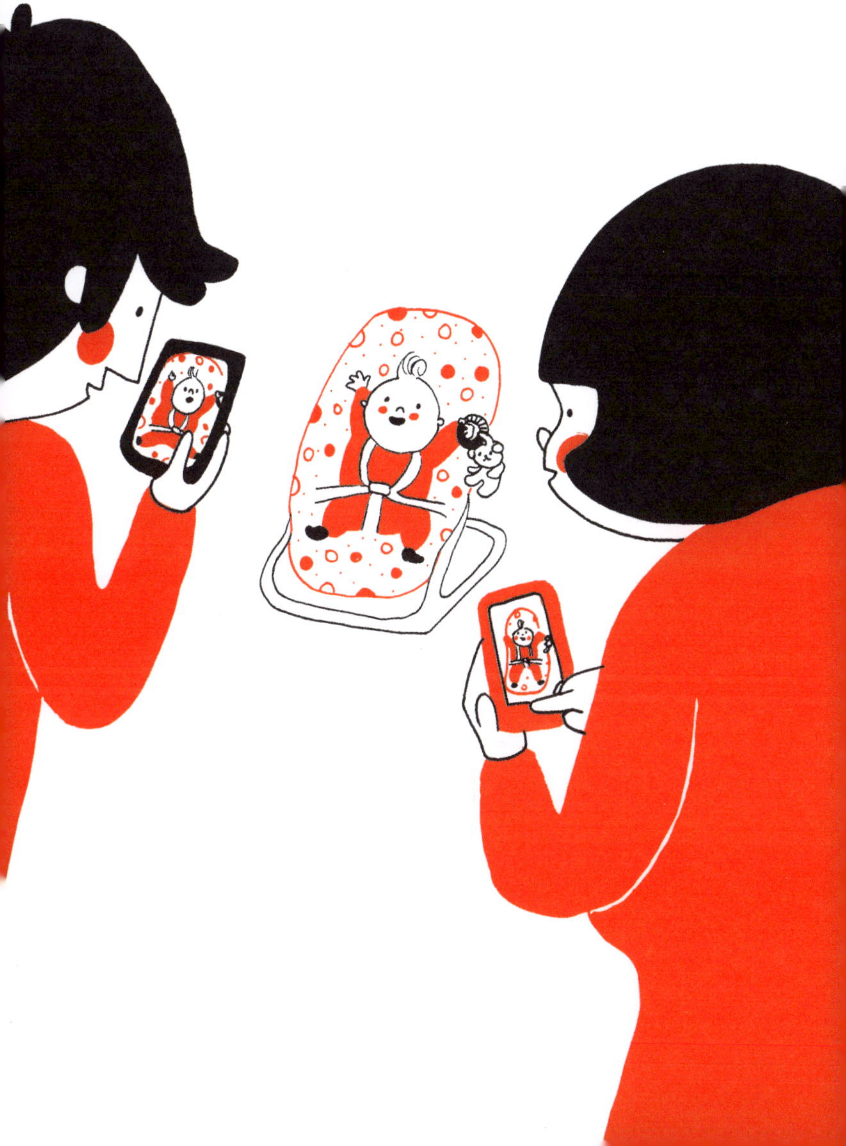

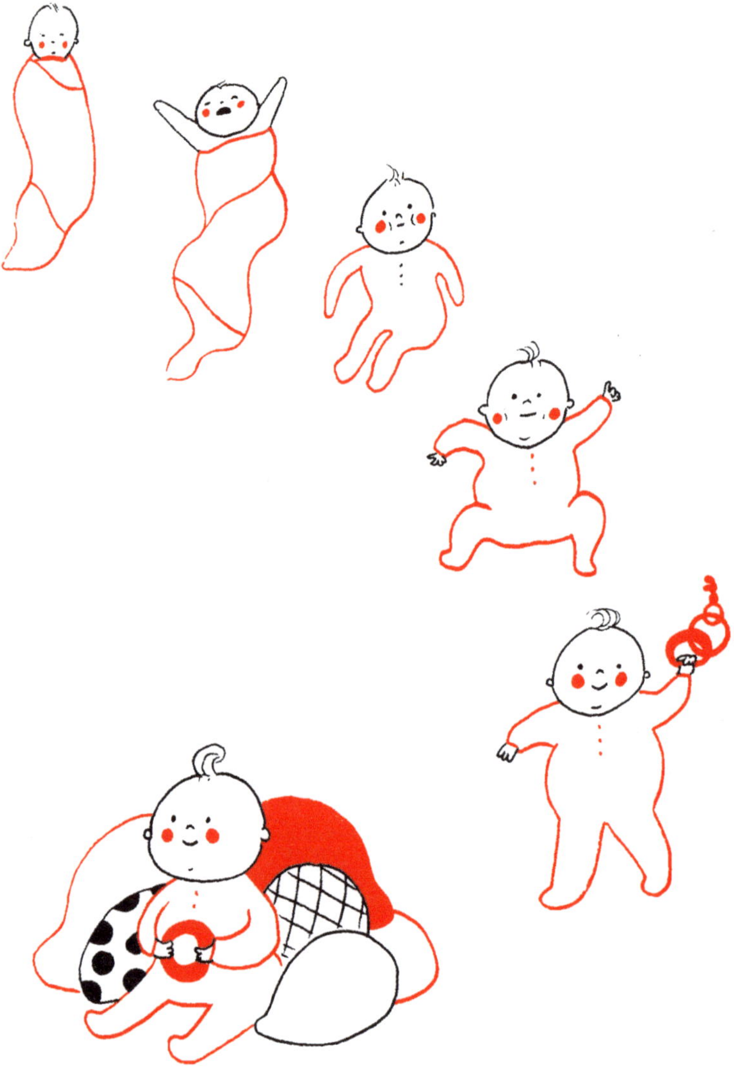

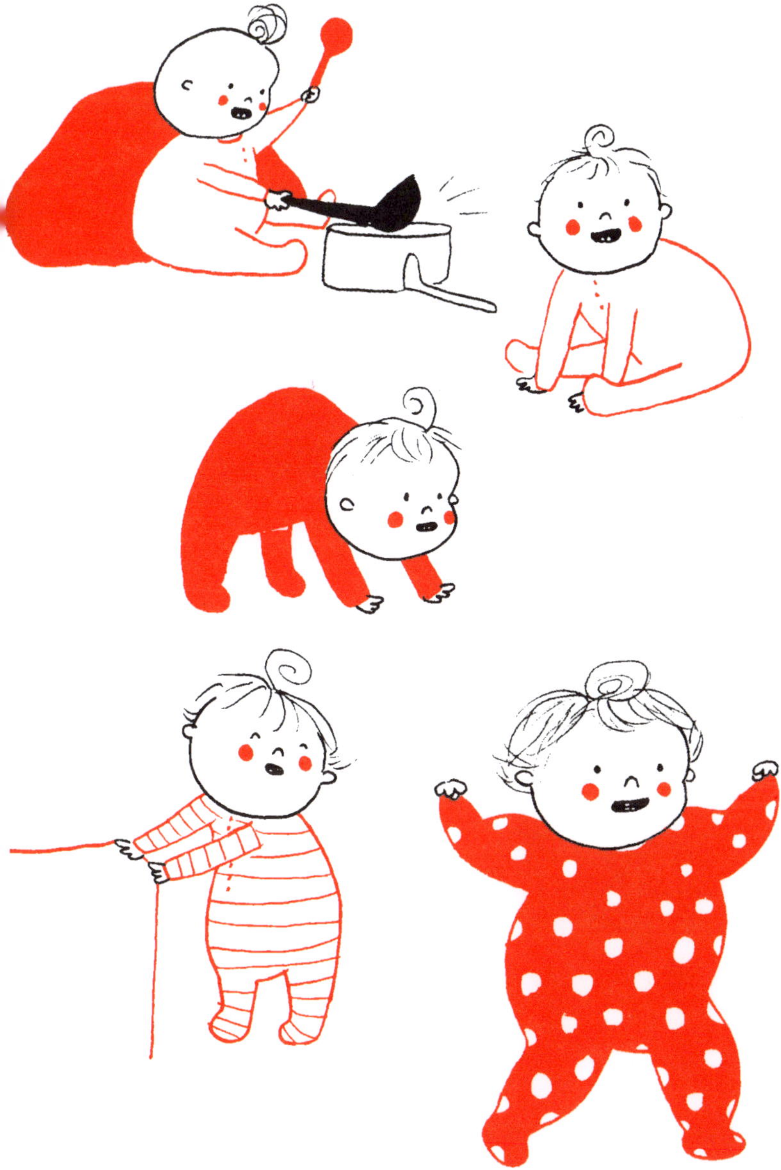

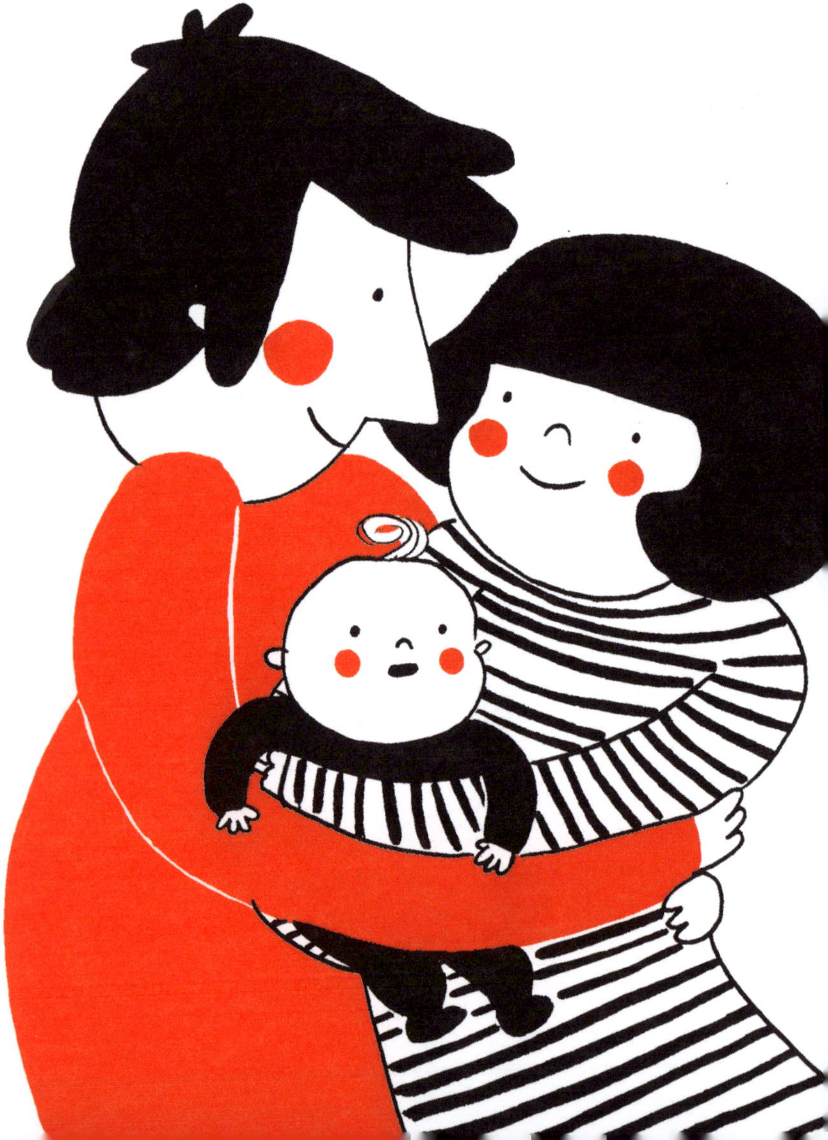

Philippa Rice is an artist who works in a number of different mediums, including comics, illustration, animation, model-making, and crochet. Her other works include SOPPY and SISTER BFFs.

Philippa grew up in London, and now she lives in Nottingham with illustrator Luke Pearson and their daughter, Robin.

Andrews McMeel Publishing
a division of Andrews McMeel Universal
1130 Walnut Street, Kansas City, Missouri 64106

www.andrewsmcmeel.com

19 20 21 22 23 TEN 10 9 8 7 6 5 4 3 2 1

ISBN: 978-1-4494-9917-4

Library of Congress Control Number: 2019933591

Attention: Schools and Businesses
Andrews McMeel books are available at quantity discounts with bulk
purchase for educational, business, or sales promotional use.
For information, please e-mail the Andrews McMeel Publishing
Special Sales Department: specialsales@amuniversal.com.

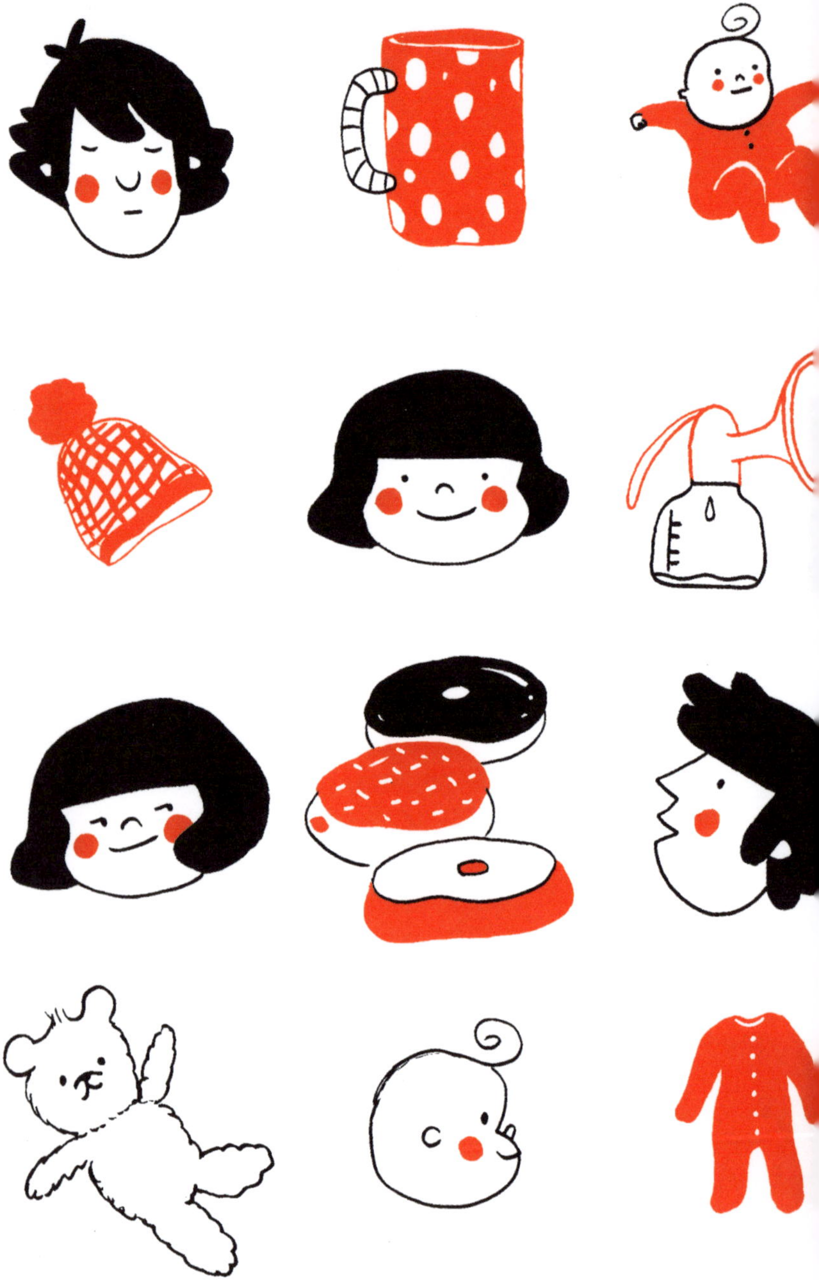